# Explosive Plyometrics

# Dr. Michael Yessis

# Explosive Plyometrics

# Dr. Michael Yessis

Published by:

Ultimate Athlete Concepts

Michigan USA

2009

For information and to order copies:

www.ultimateathleteconcepts.com

# Table of Contents

Chapter 1: Understanding Explosive Plyometrics ......................... 1

Chapter 2: Explosive Leg Training ............................................. 25

Chapter 3: Explosive Arm Training ............................................. 70

Chapter 4: Explosive Mid-Section Training ................................. 97

Chapter 5: Total Body Explosive Training .................................. 109

Chapter 6: Integration of Explosive Plyometrics ....................... 120

Chapter 7: Other Factors ........................................................... 136

About the Author ...................................................................... 143

# CHAPTER 1

# UNDERSTANDING EXPLOSIVE PLYOMETRICS

The need for explosive plyometric training becomes apparent when you examine the physical qualities needed in most sports. The main skills (actions) that you perform are done quickly and usually with great force. For example, athletes who run in their sport (soccer, football, baseball, basketball, lacrosse, rugby and track) must be fast. Pitchers, baseball and softball outfielders, shot, discus and javelin throwers must exhibit maximum speed and force in throwing.

Boxers and martial artists must be able to deliver quick and explosive punches and/or kicks. Jumps, jump shots and cuts must be executed quickly and explosively. Football, soccer, field hockey, tennis and other players must be able to exhibit quick cutting actions (agility) and fast acceleration to get to, or away from, their opponent or the ball.

If you are into archery or chess and checkers, then quickness and speed are not important. If you are a powerlifter or bodybuilder the critical factor is the amount of weight that you move or the number of sets and repetitions that you do, not speed or explosive power. All other sports require speed, quickness and/or explosive power which are determined by your strength and the speed with which it is displayed. This is where explosive plyometrics can improve your performance greatly.

## Background

Explosive plyometrics is a form of explosive training used to increase speed, quickness and power. Although this type of training has been around for over 40 years, it is only in the last decade that plyometrics has become a "buzz" word. But its application is still generally misunderstood. Many people erroneously believe that explosive plyometric, or speed-strength training as it is often called, is used mainly to develop strength, as a warm-up, or used to develop jump endurance. Some even believe it is dangerous and will cause injuries.

In reality, explosive plyometrics is needed to improve skill execution, game performance, and to prevent injury. Because most sports skills are executed in an explosive manner, you must train to duplicate these conditions in order to become a better competitive player. Thus, explosive plyometrics is a key training method that can improve your game play skills, as much as if not more than, strength or any other one type of training.

In essence, it can be said that explosive plyometrics is a method of "converting" increases in strength into speed and explosive power. It is a method that relies on bringing about a forced involuntary stretch that accumulates energy and then returns it in the muscle contraction after the stretch. The method is based on what is now known as the stretch-shorten cycle.

This concept was developed by Dr. Yuri Verkhoshansky of the former Soviet Union. He was the first to apply this concept to the training of athletes and proved it can improve performance greatly. By using this concept he developed what we now know as plyometrics.

The term plyometrics, was coined by Fred Wilt, former US track coach. When he learned of my work and how I had introduced this concept in the United States through Russian translations of Verkhoshansky's work years before, we collaborated to get this information out to all US coaches. At that time we had a lot of resistance from coaches and even doctors. In general, they believed it was too dangerous. In the meantime, unfortunately, some individuals took this information and capitalized on it by writing books and articles about plyometrics that were inaccurate. This, in turn, created great confusion.

As a result, the plyometric training most often seen in the United States is, in reality, jump training; not the original method as proposed by Dr. Verkhoshansky. Understand that jump training is a separate type of training. It is differentiated from plyometric training mainly by the amount of time taken to execute the transition from the stretch to the contraction.

For example, explosive plyometric exercises involve jumps, but all jumps are not plyometric! This misunderstanding came about because the authors of some of the more popular plyometric books and articles did not understand the difference between jump and plyometric exercises. This is why, since plyometrics was first described by these early authors, who appeared to be more interested in exploiting the concept of plyometrics, jumps and plyometrics soon became synonymous. Even today, just about any article you read calls all different types of jumps plyometrics.

As brought out earlier, jump training and plyometric training are two distinct and separate entities. This is why Dr. Yuri Verkhoshansky, known as the father of plyometrics, refuses to accept this title. In my discussions with him, he says that what we call plyometrics "is not the training that I created and have athletes use". In true (explosive) plyometrics the exercise must be executed as quickly as possible -- in

0.15 to 0.2 seconds. Jump training takes longer to execute, much longer in most cases. However, jump training is valuable and should be used in the training of athletes, especially in the early years and in preparation for explosive plyometrics.

To differentiate what is commonly called plyometrics and the method created by Dr. Verkhoshansky, we now call his method the shock method. As reported in my earlier writings in the Soviet Sports Review, I also called this method the hit method. In essence this means that when you make contact with the ground as in a jump or when receiving a ball or other object, your body experiences a shock or hit. This elicits the involuntary forced stretch during which you accumulate energy for the return action.

To learn more about plyometrics I visited Dr. Verkhoshansky in Russia several times and have been in correspondence with him since the 1980s, after I first learned of his work back in the late 1960s. In my visits he showed me several plyometric and specialized explosive exercises that he developed. Some were strictly exercises that duplicated the joint actions that the athlete must accomplish in execution of his game skills. Other exercises were called specialized or dynamic correspondence exercises. These exercises duplicate the technique seen in execution of the skill. They combine skill technique with strength and/or explosive power in one exercise to develop the physical quality as seen in competition.

Most of Verkhoshansky's plyometric work revolved around exercises for sprinters and jumpers. For examples of some of these exercises see the DVD that will accompany this book. Based on the early work done by Verkhoshansky, and with my background in sports skill biomechanics and kinesiology, I was able to develop many more explosive plyometric and specialized exercises not only for runners and jumpers but for athletes in other sports. Many of these appear in my other books such as *Explosive Running, Explosive Basketball Training* and *Women's Soccer: Using Science to Improve Speed*.

Even though jump and plyometric training involve many of the same mechanisms, they are very different in their effect on the body. For example, jump exercises involve the central nervous system (CNS) but not to the same extent as explosive plyometric exercises. In the latter case, the stress on the central nervous system is much greater and has a much more noticeable effect on the body. The eccentric strength component is also much less in jump training.

Because execution of true plyometric exercises entails strong involvement of the CNS, you should not over do plyometric workouts. This is especially true when doing maximum intensity exercises such as depth jumps. If you do too many depth jumps, you will most likely experience a disruption in your nervous system which can make you irritable and interfere with your sleep patterns. In this case less is more effective than more.

Although plyometric training is the key to success for many athletes, it is not for everyone. Youngsters especially should beware of doing explosive plyometric or very intense types of explosive plyometric training because it can be very stressful to the joints and nervous system. Most important in youth (pre- and early post-puberty) is development of strength and effective technique. Mastery of foundational strength and technique ensure rapid progress not only before, but especially after puberty. At this time your body will be ready for the high intensity training, and its effects will be the greatest. With continued training you will see accelerated improvement which becomes even more pronounced in the latter teenage and early adult years.

## Preparing for Plyometric Exercises

To prepare for true explosive plyometric training, participate in lead-up type plyometric activities, such as skipping rope, and easy hopping, jumping and leaping. These different kinds of jumps are natural activities that develop the basic elements of muscle resiliency (elasticity) and lay the base for more intense plyometric training.

To do explosive plyometric training, you must be physically prepared with an adequate strength base and good technique. This includes knowing how to jump and how to land. In addition, you must continually develop additional strength that can be used for improving your explosive power. Only doing strength training or plyometric training will not produce as good result as when plyometric (explosive) training follows strength of training. You want to increase your maximum strength levels but this does not mean doing maximum strength training with the weights in the 90 to 100% of maximum zone. Best are strength exercises in his 75 to 85% of maximum zone.

Strength plays a major role in explosive plyometric training but by itself, is not the key quality that determines your success in speed or power (speed plus strength) oriented sports. The only exceptions to this is pre-adolescence and early adolescence, or if you never strength trained before. For athletes who have been involved in strength training for several or more years, strength must be coupled with speed to be most beneficial. Only in this way can your strength be used to its greatest advantage. If not, gaining too much strength (without speed or plyometric training) can cause a decrease in speed and explosiveness.

Because of the high intensity of explosive plyometric exercises and the effect they have on the CNS, explosive plyometric exercises should only be done in the specialized period of training. Lead up jumps which include easy skipping, jumping and hopping, can be done in the general preparatory period (GPP) and year-round for various effects. For example, lead up jumps are great for warm-up prior to doing explosive plyometrics.

In the specialized period of training, explosive plyometric jumps should come as close as possible to duplicating what occurs in the joint actions seen in execution of your sport. For example, ankle jumps are very effective in the specialized period of training as they duplicate the ankle joint action seen in running and jumping. Note that in order to duplicate what occurs in these two skills, the jumps must be maximal with full ankle joint extension. Thus, as you go through the various plyometric exercises, look for those that duplicate the actions that you must execute during game performance. In this way you'll get maximum value out of the plyometric training.

To better understand what is involved in explosive plyometric training, you must understand the stretch-shortening concept or simply, the stretch reflex as developed and expanded upon by Dr. Verkhoshansky. It is the key factor involved in execution of explosive plyometrics. It seems like a simple concept today but it was revolutionary when first proposed by Verkhoshansky. It became the key to execution of explosive plyometric exercises as well as many dynamic correspondence type exercises, also known as conjugate or specialized strength and/or explosive exercises.

## The Stretch Reflex

Learning how to use the stretch reflex when doing certain exercises can bring about great development of the fast twitch muscle fibers. This entails a quick, high intensity muscle contraction. Keep in mind that there are basically four types of muscle fibers. Most are slow twitch (ST) and fast twitch (FT) fibers. The ST fibers are slow contracting and slow to fatigue. They are efficient in sustaining prolonged low intensity activity and are used extensively in the endurance sports and to a limited extent in bodybuilding and powerlifting.

At the same time, maximal muscle power output and the potential for explosive movement is determined mainly by the proportion of FT fibers. For example, weightlifters and sprinters who do more explosive movements have a considerably higher proportion of fast twitch fibers than bodybuilders, powerlifters and endurance athletes. ==High intensity is not necessarily dependent upon the use of near-maximal or maximal loads, but more to the degree to which the relevant muscle fibers are recruited during the effort.==

The terms "fast twitch" and "slow twitch" do not necessarily mean that fast movements recruit exclusively FT fibers or slow movements only ST fibers. The kind and number of fibers involved are determined by the force that is produced and the duration of work.

For example, the maximum force generated during rapid acceleration of a 220 pound bench press can easily exceed the maximum force produced during a slowly accelerated 330 pound bench press. Both a small load accelerated rapidly and a heavy load accelerated slowly strongly involve the FT fibers. But the explosive movements as seen in speed and power sports also rely heavily on the action of the FT fibers in fast movements.

Accelerated movements recruit the muscle stretch (myotatic) reflex which elicits a faster and more powerful contraction. The pre-stretch principle is well known in sports and in the plyometric method of explosive training. In essence, the muscle/tendon must be placed on stretch before the concentric contraction. The faster this happens and the more forcefully it happens, the stronger the acceleration.

Fast twitch fibers are the main contributors to force production in fast ballistic movements while the slow twitch fibers make their major contribution during very slow movements. FT fiber action can be impaired by the growth of slow twitch fibers since they appear to have a dampening effect on FT contractions during quick or fast movements. Thus, even though heavy resistance training serves as a powerful stimulus for the development and hypertrophy of both slow twitch and fast twitch fibers, FT fiber development requires special training.

Training the fast twitch fibers with explosive plyometrics involves the storage and release of elastic energy by the connective tissues in the muscle/tendon complex. This is done by involving the stretch reflex, which entails accumulation of energy in the muscle-tendon complex prior to a quick explosive contraction that accelerates the weight or object held. After this, the weight or object moves on its own momentum followed by some muscle involvement to eventually stop the movement.

When using the stretch reflex the muscles do not react in the same manner as during a slow movement. During slow movements the main muscles involved in performing the movement as well as their antagonists, undergo contraction to control the movement via feedback over the full range of motion. To use the stretch reflex to get a more explosive contraction you must program it in advance.

The bench press can be used to illustrate how the stretch reflex is used to elicit a more powerful muscle contraction. Begin the exercise with the arms straight, fully extended above the chest and holding a barbell. Lower the barbell at a normal rate of speed and as you approach the bottom position, before touching the chest, quickly change directions to accelerate the barbell upward. In essence, you blast out of the bottom position and then allow the barbell to continue movement on its own inertia. After this you use the muscles to completely extend the arms if needed.

To do the exercise it is important that you inhale and hold the breath as you lower the barbell and execute the explosive change and acceleration phase from the bottom position. Exhale after the barbell has passed the most difficult portion of the lift or when the arms are extended. The breath holding is needed during explosive movements to stabilize the trunk for safety and to ensure effective execution.

When the bench press is executed using the stretch reflex, there is much greater force created in the initial pushing phase. The reason for this is that you use the energy accumulated on the down movement to execute the switch and upward acceleration of the barbell. Keep in mind that as you lower the barbell the triceps, pectorals and anterior deltoids undergo an eccentric contraction during which the muscles lengthen and become more tense. This muscle tension increases as you lower the bar and is then used to stop the downward movement.

After this the muscle contraction switches to a brief isometric contraction when the movement stops, and then the even greater eccentric muscle tension switches into the concentric contraction with which you accelerate the barbell upward. All this takes place in hundredths of a second! The eccentric contraction tension is most important for eliciting the stretch reflex and for controlling the barbell on the down phase.

Simply stated, the muscles stretch on the lowering phase and the tension generated is used in the muscle contraction to quickly raise the barbell. The stretch reflex allows you to not only use the strength of the muscles involved but also the energy accumulated on the down phase to enable you to generate even more power, using mainly the FT fibers. If you pause for a second in the bottom position, as often occurs in a slow movement, the energy gained in the eccentric contraction will be dissipated in the form of heat. As a result, you will have to generate additional concentric strength to push the barbell back up.

The quick switch from the eccentric to the concentric contraction is analogous to bouncing a super ball or other resilient type ball. When you toss the ball downward and it makes contact with the ground, the ball undergoes deformation which compresses the air and/or material on the inside, creating greater pressure. This is analogous to the muscle developing greater tension during the eccentric contraction as the weight is being lowered. The built-up pressure inside the ball then returns the ball to its original or slightly elongated shape as it leaves the ground (rebounds) upward to almost the same height without additional force being added. This equates to the release of energy stored in the eccentric contraction.

Phil Murphy, former lineman on the then Los Angeles Rams football team in the early 80"s is a great example of what can be accomplished with explosive training using the stretch reflex. Phil, who was already extremely strong, was brought to me for quickness and explosive training. He weighed 352 pounds and stood about 6'4". After approximately seven weeks of training, Phil lost 25 pounds of mostly fat and posted 255 pounds of lean muscle mass at a weight of 325. This is more muscle than I have ever seen on any athlete. In testing done by the team, he was equal to, if not superior to, all the other linemen (who weighed around 280) in the 10-20 yard dashes, and in the agility test. He was so powerful, he was able to able to leap up onto a three foot table from a push-up position.

Exercises that use the stretch reflex, are ballistic in nature and are perfectly safe and effective. However, they cannot be done on exercise machines as they do not allow you to repeat the movement with a pre-stretch. If you do explosive movements on a typical exercise machine, the weight stack, just as a free weight, develops momentum during the lowering and raising phases. When you quickly change directions, the momentum of the weights keeps them moving in sometimes the opposite direction from which they should be going. This, in turn, may bind the cable and the cable may leave the pulley or even break because of the great tension built up on the quick switch.

To ensure that the movements are done safely, it is important to have the necessary eccentric strength to control the weights on the down phase and to generate the tension needed to make the quick switch and utilize the stretch reflex. To provide safety use about 50-75% of the usual training weight (or body weight) used for a typical set. The lighter weight allows you to make a quicker switch in direction.

If the weight or force developed is extremely great, you will have co-contraction of the agonist and antagonist muscles and you will not be able to make a quick switch to quickly accelerate the weight or body. The key to utilizing the stretch reflex is to generate maximum tension in the eccentric contraction with relative relaxation of the opposing muscles except as needed to keep the joint stable. If the opposing muscles are strongly contracted, they will not allow you to make a quick switch.

The weights (resistance) should not be too light in order to prevent excessive momentum, which may keep the weights moving beyond the normal range of motion of the joint. When the weight is light and moving fast it may be difficult for the muscles to stop the movement. In this case, you should use medicine balls or other objects so they can be released to dissipate the momentum.

The stretch reflex is incorporated in all explosive plyometric exercises, especially those that involve the extensor muscles, which usually contain a greater proportion of fast twitch fibers. For example, it can be used in a squat, overhead press (or jerk or push-press), triceps press, bench press, trunk rotation, medial shoulder joint rotation and others.

In the squat, as in the other exercises, different down positions can be used from which to execute the quick switch. For example, stop before reaching the thigh level position and then leap upward. Do a one quarter to one half squat to approximately a 145 degree knee joint angle and then quickly change directions to return to the standing position or leave the ground. In all cases, however, the descent should be smooth and under control while the switch and return is executed quickly—as though shot out of a cannon.

Understand that using the stretch reflex does not mean a bouncing rebound. There is no bouncing as you approach the position for the quick reversal. You merely make a quick change from the down movement to the up movement. You do not give the muscles a chance to lose the tension generated as when you relax or hold the down position even momentarily.

When doing exercises involving the stretch reflex, it is usually best to stop after a complete repetition. Doing this gives you a chance to mentally and physically prepare for the next repetition. Keep in mind that you must think out the movements in advance so that as you execute the exercise, you will be prepared for the quick switch and will be able to execute it in a timely and explosive manner. In some cases you can use quick, short repetitions but no more than five-six reps maximum.

To get the most out of the stretch reflex, the muscles and nervous system should be fresh. Thus, explosive plyometric exercises should always be done at the beginning of training, after you have undergone a vigorous warm-up to prepare the muscles for this work. When fatigue sets in, do not do explosive plyometrics. At this time the eccentric contraction is not as strong as needed and you may not be able to control the weight either on the down or up phases. The greater the levels of fatigue, the less the muscle resiliency and the more prone you become to injury.

# Biomechanical Factors Involved

Explosive plyometric (speed-strength) exercises involve basic biomechanical mechanisms. For example, in leg or arm jumping, the magnitude of the force generated on a landing depends on the height (distance) you travel before touchdown. In this case gravity is the force that accelerates you toward the ground.

When receiving a moving object, as, for example, a medicine ball coming at you, the force when you make contact with the ball, depends on ball weight and the speed with which the ball is moving. When the ball is moving horizontally rather than downward, gravity is not a major force with which you must contend.

In this case, you must be able to handle the force generated by the ball or other object due to its velocity or momentum which takes into consideration ball weight. The greater its initial acceleration and the less the distance that the ball must travel, the greater is the force you experience at contact. The further the ball travels the more gravity pulls down on it and the greater the air resistance to slow down the ball. However, because the action ends so quickly in a typical exercise you will hardly notice these changes.

In jumping with the legs or arms, ground reaction forces as well as the amount of time it takes in transition from the down to the up phase, varies greatly among the different types of jumps. In general, the faster the transition, the more explosive and the higher (or longer) will be the jump. In an easy jump, landing and take-off times are much longer. When receiving a moving object or when jumping, the reaction forces of your legs, body or arms depend upon the eccentric strength of the muscles to quickly stop the forward moving ball or body in a jump down.

**The Jump.** To better understand what happens in a plyometric jump involving the legs, following is a description of the sequential muscle and joint actions that are involved:

When you are airborne and dropping down toward the ground, you body has kinetic energy i.e., a force created by gravity pulling you downward. The higher the height, the faster your speed (and force) upon contact with the ground because your body accelerates as it drops toward the ground. Upon making touchdown, which should be ball-heel almost immediately, there is some absorption of the landing forces to cushion the landing. But, most of the forces experienced must be withstood and accumulated for another jump upward.

It is important that you land on a resilient surface. If you jump on a grassy field there is some give in the grass and earth, making such jumps relatively safe. If you jump on a gym floor the floorboards have some "give" to cushion the landing forces. Do not jump on concrete, unless you use a resilient mat or padding so that there is some "give" to the surface. When you first start jump training (as a lead-up to plyometric training) use "soft" surfaces to land on. More advanced jumpers with better technique and higher levels of strength use firmer surfaces.

Upon landing there is some absorption of the landing forces, mainly for safety, beginning with the plantar surface (sole) of the foot, followed by ankle, knee, hip and spinal joint flexion. As the joints undergo flexion and the muscles and tendons lengthen (stretch) they develop tension in the eccentric contraction. When the tension becomes sufficiently great, downward movement stops. The muscles switch to a momentary isometric contraction and then to the concentric contraction to propel you back up in the air together with the give back of energy by the tendons and other connective issues as they shorten from their elongated state.

Note that is not only the muscles that undergo a stretch and contraction. The tendons also play a very important role, especially the Achilles tendon of the shin and the tendons on the bottom of the foot. These are very resilient structures that can withstand and accumulate great amounts of tension when they are forcefully stretched to store energy and then give it back in the take-off. The amount of energy return can be 60-70% of the landing forces!

Because an explosive plyometric jump landing and take-off is executed quickly, the muscles do not have time to experience a volitional contraction to generate the force needed for a conventional stationary take off. Usually the volitional contraction time takes up to 0.6 to 0.8 sec while an explosive jump takes place in 0.1-0.2 sec.

This is possible because of the pre-tension of the muscle and support structures in the eccentric contraction. Without pre-tensing the muscles it is impossible to execute a quick (explosive) jump.

In the landing there is forced loading of the muscles. This happens automatically. To help prepare for the forces generated on landing, you must engage the brain prior to touchdown. In essence, you alert the muscles to prepare for the landing. The brain sends signals to the corresponding muscles and joints so that as soon as touchdown occurs the muscles that are already pre-tensed can immediately handle the landing forces to prevent you from "sinking" or lowering the body too much. Keep in mind that the lower the body goes on landing, the longer it takes for the body to come up and the longer it takes for the jump to be executed.

The biomechanical factors involved in leg jumping are the same for arm jumping. The only difference is that the landing or touchdown in arm jumping is made on the fingers and palm of the hand, followed by hyperextension in the wrist joint, flexion in the elbow joint, and flexion or abduction in the shoulder joint. The exact action depends on whether your elbow is alongside your body or out to the side.

Because the hand, wrist, elbow and shoulder joint muscles are much smaller than those of the corresponding joints in the leg, the jump is usually not very high. However, some athletes with explosive arms are capable of jumping from the push-up position with only the arms up to a height of two-three feet.

As brought out earlier, before undertaking an explosive plyometric training, you must have a well established strength base. You must have the needed concentric, eccentric, and isometric strength since all of these muscle contraction regimes are included in plyometric training. Understand that the force developed in some types of explosive plyometric exercises can reach up to 20 times your body weight; thus you must have sufficient strength and good technique to withstand such forces. In addition, it is necessary to develop strength in a manner that duplicates as closely as possible, what you must do in your sport.

## Breathing When Doing Plyometrics

How you breathe plays an important role in regard to getting maximum results from plyometric exercises. Most important is to hold your breath on exertion – that is, on the hardest part of the exercise, when you are overcoming resistance in the switch from the down or receiving phase to the up or repelling phase. You then exhale on the return or after completion of the exercise while staying in control of the movements. But don't be surprised if you read or hear the opposite from other sources – that you should exhale on exertion and inhale on completion.

Inhaling and holding the breath briefly on the eccentric to concentric muscle contraction switch and concentric phase or on any exertion in any sport, comes naturally. Many studies have shown that whenever athletic skills are executed properly, you hold your breath on the exertion – during the power phase – when maximum force is generated. The breath-holding is especially important when exhibiting a maximum strength or explosive (plyometric) act. Inhaling and holding the breath on exertion provides up to 20 percent greater force and stabilizes the spine, which in turn, prevents lower back injuries. It transforms the trunk into a stable unit against which your arms and/or legs can act more effectively.

The need to hold your breath can even be inferred from the recommendations given for relaxation. In order to relax, you inhale and then exhale. As you exhale, the muscles relax. In essence, exhalation is associated with relaxation.

Inhalation and then exhalation helps you relax before starting a race, executing a free throw, shooting an arrow or firearm, and other skills. But before starting a dynamic skill it is important that the muscles have some tension – not excessive tension, but sufficient tension to execute the skill with force. Thus, inhalation and breath-holding are needed immediately before and during execution of the key power actions. Studies done with monitoring of breathing patterns have proven this beyond any doubt.

In effective breathing, do not inhale to your maximum capacity and then hold it. Doing this can make you very uncomfortable. Just take a breath slightly greater than usual and then hold it to experience the positive benefits. This is especially important for stabilizing the body, holding the spine in position, and getting greater power and accuracy in your skill execution or explosives plyometric exercise. The power phase is very short. Thus, you do not hold your breath too long.

# CHAPTER 2

# EXPLOSIVE LEG TRAINING

Explosive legs are the key to jump height, running speed and kicking force. Because of the similarity of joint actions involved in execution of running, jumping and kicking, the same explosive plyometric exercises can greatly improve performance in these skills. However, there are also some very specific exercises for each of these skills for which the training must be differentiated, especially for the higher level athlete.

## Active Stretches

Before doing explosive exercises, it is important that you have an adequate warm-up. The muscles must be ready for the vigorous activity involved. Because of this, you should do active stretches to stimulate and prepare the muscles that will be involved in the exercises. Active stretches not only stretch the muscles and tissues but prepare the muscles for the action by activating and warming them up.

Do not do slow, static stretches in which you hold a stretch for extended periods of time. They can be detrimental to the joints if held too long, and most importantly, do not prepare the muscles for action. They do the opposite, they figuratively put the muscles to sleep in a relaxed state and do not prepare them for action, especially explosive actions. As a result, you become weaker and do worse in your performance!

Some of the best active stretches for the leg and hip joints are:
1. *The classic (Russian) lunge (long stride, trunk erect, rear leg straight but relaxed) to stretch the hip flexors.*
2. *Classic side lunge (long stride, trunk erect, side push-off leg straight but relaxed) to stretch the groin (adductors).*
3. *Good Morning (arched back, forward bend over) to stretch the hamstrings.*
4. *Squat (to the thigh level or lower position) to stretch the quadriceps.*
5. *Calf stretch (heel lowering and raising on a raised platform or from a forward leaning position on the ground) to stretch the Achilles tendon.*

# General Jumping

The ability to jump well is very important in plyometric training. Although, jumping is a universal skill and is usually considered "natural," it does not mean that everyone has an effective jump. You can improve your technique and physical ability to execute a quicker and higher jump.

Many coaches and athletes believe that either you are a jumper or you are not. Some have even characterized the ability to jump according to race, as typified by the statement, "white men can't jump." However, jumping can be improved greatly through better technique and doing the right exercises in the correct manner. Adding up to 12 inches is not unheard of and most athletes can put at least 4-6 inches on their jumps.

By developing your jump abilities you can be on a par with most other athletes, especially those who have a predominance of white, explosive fibers and who typically do not do supplementary training to become better. Because of this, you can be equal to, and in many cases superior to, jumpers who are genetically predisposed. The key is to develop proper technique and have effective physical conditioning.

# Keys to Effective Jumping

## *The take-off*

Before jumping upward you must go downward into a partial squat (counter movement). As you reach the lowest point in your squat (which should be minimal), you immediately change directions. You contract the hip joint extensor muscles to raise the trunk and simultaneously with the raising of the trunk, whip the arms down and then upward. Doing this creates greater tension in the leg muscles so that as your raise the arms and trunk, the body actually becomes "lighter," but the muscles still contract more forcefully.

As the arms and trunk are being raised the knee joints extend to straighten the legs followed by ankle joint extension. Even though there is a sequence of these actions, they overlap one another. See Figure 1: E-J.

At the very end of the take-off, when the body is completely extended, only ankle joint extension takes place. As you leave the ground the legs should be fully extended (straight), and the trunk should be straight, in line with the legs (Figure 1-J). The arms are either overhead or shoulder level depending on the type and purpose of the jump.

# Figure 1: Jump Form

A  B  C  D

E  F  G  H

I  J  K  L

M  N  O  P

### *The Landing (Touchdown)*

When landing, your feet should be directly under the hips so that the landing forces can be handled efficiently by the leg muscles. Landing should take place on the balls of the feet followed immediately by the heels (whole foot), followed in turn by ankle, knee and hip joint flexion. Do not land with the toes pointed so that you land on the ball of the foot close to the toe area. Doing this can cause excessive jamming of the foot bones and create various foot problems. See Figure 1: A- D.

For a safe and effective touchdown you should land almost flat footed so that the ball-heel contact occurs very quickly. This allows for the arch of the foot to do the initial shock absorbing and more importantly, withstanding of the landing forces. The arch of the foot plays a very important role not only in the landing but also in the take-off. Thus, how you land is critical not only to good jumping ability but for prevention of injury.

Before touchdown, begin to tense the muscles. When you do this, as soon as you make initial contact, the muscles and tendons are engaged immediately and they keep you from going too low by withstanding the forces more efficiently.

*Jump Stance*

In the initial stance your feet should be directly under the hips so that when you straighten your legs they push the hips and upper body straight upward. If you place your feet wider than hip width apart, when your legs extend, the forces created will criss-cross your body. As a result only a portion of the forces will be used to raise your body; the remaining force will be wasted since it goes sideways in opposite directions to cancel one another.

A hip-width stance is also needed in execution of many exercises. For example, when you do the squat the feet should be directly under the hips. If the feet are placed wide, as in a sumo squat, you can handle more weight but the actual amount of force that you will be able to use, i.e., that will be specific to jumping, is much less. In exercises such as the good morning, placing your feet hip width apart insures a stronger stretch of the hamstring muscles than when the feet are wider apart.

## Exercise Guidelines

Do mainly those exercises that are specific to your sport or event. In the early stages select 2-3 exercises and execute one set of 6-10 repetitions each. As you develop the ability to do the exercises easily and effectively, add more exercises and sets to the training sessions. In general, do no more than six plyometric jump exercises in a session, especially when done for 2-3 sets each. Use weights in some of the exercises only after you have mastered the exercises without additional resistance.

## *EXPLOSIVE JUMP EXERCISES*

### 1. Skip (power) jumps

**Purpose**: This exercise is used to coordinate the leg push-off with the knee drive which is needed in running and in various jumps. This includes the high jump, long jump, pole vault, basketball lay-up and others.

**Execution**: Begin by taking a few preliminary steps and then push off the ground with one leg and, at the same time, drive the opposite knee forward and upward. When you leave the ground, the push-off leg and foot should be fully extended and the swing leg thigh should approach level or above and the shin should be vertical and relaxed. Land on the take-off leg and then take a short skip and repeat using the opposite leg for the push-off and knee drive respectively. Distance and speed of forward movement are not important in this exercise, concentrate on a combination of maximum vertical height and forward distance. (See Figure 2.1, A-C)

**Figure 2.1: Skip (power) Jumps**

A          B          C

2. **Double leg jumps in place**

**Purpose:** For greater power on vertical take-offs, and preparation for a good, safe landing. It is needed to acquire good jump height, quickness and speed.

**Execution:** Assume a standing position with the feet directly under the hips. Bend the legs slightly, swing the arms down and around and leap up as high as possible with full extension of the legs. Make sure the legs are straight and toes are pointed on takeoff. On touchdown, land close to the arch of the foot, i.e. on the ball and then heel almost simultaneously. Execute the landing and take-off as quickly as possible. Prepare yourself mentally and physically for landing and takeoff. (See Figure 2.2, A-C)

**Note:** To increase the difficulty and to develop even greater explosive power, hold a dumbbell in each hand as you execute the double leg jumps. Keep the arms flexed and control the weights as you do the jump so that the dumbbells do not bang into the body.

**Figure 2.2: Double Leg Jump in Place**

A          B          C

3. **Double leg jumps for height and distance.**

   **Purpose:** When you have mastered the in-place jumps, do the double leg jumps for height and distance. Use this exercise to learn to how direct your forces mainly upward but slightly forward as needed for good jump height, quickness and speed.

**Execution:** Execution is the same as in #2 except in the takeoff you incline your body slightly forward so that after you leap up you will come down approximately 12-18 inches from the place of takeoff. (See Figure 2.3, A-D)

**Figure 2.3: Double leg jumps for height and distance**

A  B  C  D

4. **Double leg jumps for height and slight forward movement with a 90° turn.**

   **Purpose:** This is an advanced form of exercise #3 that works on not only jump explosiveness and height but also develops greater coordination of the body and limbs when airborne. Attention must be paid to the landing so that it is on both feet approximately hip to shoulder width apart. It is needed in all sports that require execution of skills while airborne. This includes the basketball jump shot, volleyball spike, basketball and volleyball blocking, pass receiving or breaking up passes in football and in baseball field catching.

**Execution:** Jump upward the same as in the vertical jump for height and forward movement. When you are airborne, rotate your body 90° to the left or right. Land facing sideways and then immediately leap up again and rotate back to the front facing position. On the next jump rotate in the same direction 90° and then rotate to the front facing position on the next jump. (See Figure 2.4, A-F)

After you have completed a set of 10 jumps, do the exercise with rotation to the opposite side. As you do this exercise be sure that your body moves forward in a straight line. If you find yourself moving off the line it indicates that your coordination is not as good as it could be, or that your jumps are angled in the take-off. Check to make sure that your jumps are directly vertical, with only slight forward movement.

**Figure 2.4: Double leg jumps for height with a 90° turn**

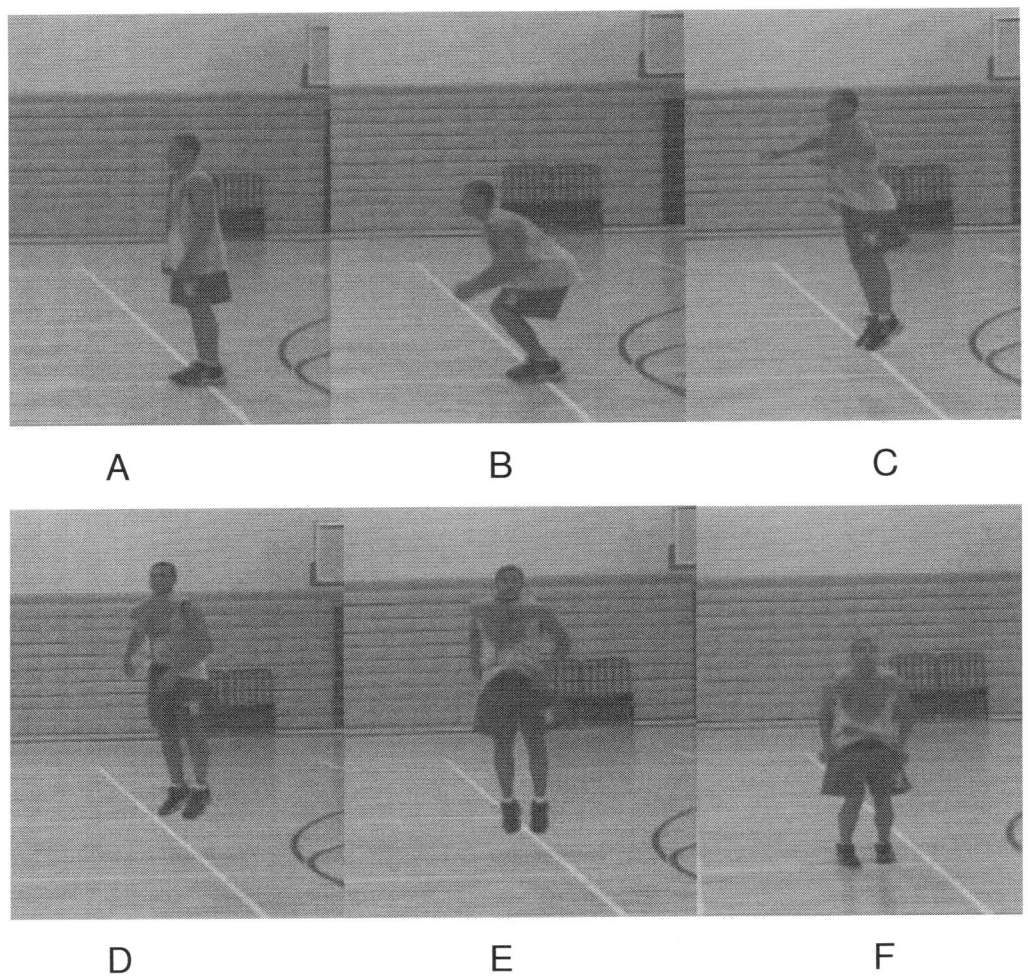

A            B            C

D            E            F

5. **Double leg jumps with a 180° turn**

   **Purpose:** This jump is more difficult than the jump with a 90° turn, and requires a higher level of coordination. In addition, you must have ample jump height to give you enough time to execute the full 180° turn prior to the landing. This exercise is important in basketball, football, volleyball, soccer and the high jump.

**Execution:** Execute in the same manner as the jump with a 90° turn, except you make a 180° turn on each jump. After leaping straight up in a front facing position, execute a 180° so that you land facing backwards. Leap up again and immediately execute another 180° turn to land facing front. Execute your turns in the same direction on each turn, or rotate the body in a full circle after two jumps. After completing the jumps with a turn in one direction, execute them again going in the opposite direction. (See Figure 2.5, A-F)

**Figure 2.5: Double leg jumps for height with a 180° turn**

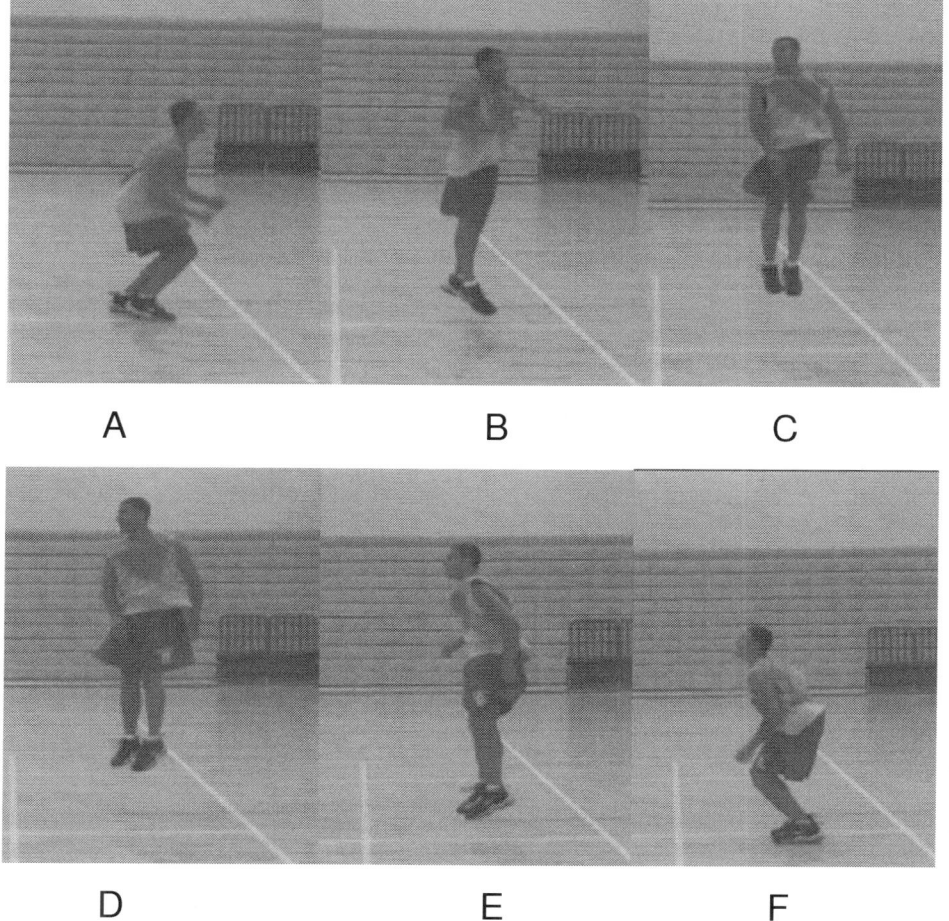

A  B  C

D  E  F

6. **Tuck jumps**

   **Purpose:** The purpose of tuck jumps is to work on a strong vertical push-off with slight forward movement while simultaneously bringing the knees up into a tuck position. This exercise is important when jumping over various barriers and hurdles. However, it is not recommended for most athletes as it may teach incorrect jump technique. Be sure that your legs are fully extended and the toes pointed after leaving the ground and before bringing the knees up to go into a tuck position.

   **Execution:** The jump is executed as in the above exercises. You should have completely extended legs with the toes pointed as you take off from the ground. After take-off when you are airborne, bring the knees up quickly until they are about chest high, then bring the legs down to a straight body position and prepare for the landing. Take off quickly immediately after landing. (See Figure 2.6, A-D)

   Tuck jumps can also be practiced by jumping over low height objects or barriers as well as jumping up onto boxes. However, and this is very important, do not sacrifice jump technique so that you can get the knees up in ample time. I find too many athletes doing this to get "high" and in the process they do not leap up as high as possible. Because of this I do not recommend this type of jumping because it can teach poor take-off technique. But if your take-offs are executed well, tuck jumps can serve an important purpose.

**Figure 2.6: Tuck Jumps**

A　　　　　B　　　　　C　　　　　D

7. **Single leg jumps in place**

**Purpose:** To improve your ability to land and take off on one leg. The key to successful execution of this exercise is to leap up as high as possible in a vertical direction and to execute the landing and take-off as quickly as possible. This exercise is needed in all sports that require jumping or take off on one leg as in running.

**Execution:** Stand on one leg in a well balanced position. When you are ready, swing your arms down, around and up and at the same time, drive the free leg knee upward. As the arms and free knee are driven upward fully straighten the support leg and strongly extend the ankle joint to leap up as high as possible. Prepare for the landing as described earlier and as soon as you make ground contact, cushion, withstand and execute another quick jump upward. (See Figure 2.7, A-D)

**Figure 2.7: Single Leg Jumps in Place**

A　　　　　　B　　　　　　　C　　　　　　D

8. **Single leg jumps with forward movement**

   **Purpose**: Single leg jumps with forward movement are used to direct the forces upward and forward. These actions are needed in many game situations especially in basketball, football and soccer and in all sports that require jumping.

   **Execution**: Execute in the same way as the single leg standing jump but direct the forces slightly forward on each jump. You should land approximately 12-18 inches in front of the initial take-off point. (See Figure 2.8, A-D)

**Figure 2.8: Single leg jumps with forward movement**

A    B    C    D

9. **Ankle jumps**

   **Purpose**: To emphasize the ankle joint extension. This is a key action for greater jump height, running speed and quick moves on the court of field.

   **Execution**: Assume a standing position with the feet directly under the hips. Jump with as much ankle joint extension as possible. The height will not be great since it is necessary to eliminate the knee joint as much as possible. The range of motion in the knee joint should be no more than 10-20° while the ankle joint goes through the full range of motion (about 45-60°). The toes should be pointed downward on every jump and the legs should be straight on take-off. (See Figure 2.9, A-D)

**Figure 2.9: Ankle Jumps**

A   B   C   D

10. **Double leg jumps for height and distance (bounding)**

   **Purpose**: To develop the ability to execute explosive take-offs on both legs in a forward direction. The key is to concentrate mainly on distance with some height.

   **Execution**: Execute as a regular double leg take-off jump so that the body and legs are fully extended on take-off. The body should be directed at about a 45 degree angle forward on takeoff. Upon landing, execute the next take-off as quickly as possible. If you find yourself sinking too low and the jump taking too long, cut down on the distance. This exercise is sometimes done with a tuck after the jump. (See Figure 2.10, A-D)

**Figure 2.10: Bounding**

A  B  C  D

**11. Leaping**

**Purpose**: This exercise is very beneficial in running and developing the ability to take a quick first step when accelerating and when lunging or reaching for a ball as in soccer, basketball, volleyball and other sports. When executed well, it improves coordination of a low push-off and the knee drive as needed in sprinting.

**Execution**: Take a few approach steps and then leap forward as far as possible taking off on one leg. The swing leg should be bent at the knee and driven forward at the same time as the push-off takes place. The body should remain as low as possible in the take-off and flight phase. As you prepare for the landing, sweep the forward leg down and back to once again push yourself forward as forcefully as possible. Be sure your trunk is erect and that the body is well in front of the push-off leg when ground contact is broken so that the forces are directed horizontally. (See Figure 2.11, A-C)

**CAUTION:** Do not confuse this exercise with what some coaches call bounding. In bounding, the take-off is more vertical and your body does not remain low to the ground.

**Figure 2.11: Leaping**

A             B             C

12. **Double leg side jumps**

**Purpose**: This exercise is important for improving your ability to execute lateral movements which are the key to successful cutting actions as needed in almost all team, dual and individual sports.

**Execution**: Assume a standing position with your feet together directly under the body. When ready, go into a slight crouch and leap out to one side and immediately upon landing and slightly cushioning the body, push off and leap to the opposite side. The key is to keep the head and shoulders in basically the same position and to switch the lower body from side to side.

Execute powerful movements so that you stay low and go far. If you find yourself sinking too much on each landing, or taking too long to jump back, then the distance is too great. The key is to be able to execute these jumps as quickly and as forcefully as possible while still covering maximum distance. (See Figure 2.12, A-D)

**Note:** To increase the difficulty and to develop even greater explosive power, hold a dumbbell in each hand as you execute the double leg side jumps. Keep the arms flexed to help control the weights as you do the jump so that the dumbbells do not bang into the body.

**Figure 2.12: Double leg side jumps**

A          B          C          D

13. **Single leg side jumps**

   **Purpose**: To duplicate more closely what occurs when cutting laterally. This exercise also improves your quickness in side movements.

   **Execution**: Assume a standing position with your feet together or hip width apart. When ready, flex the legs slightly and then push off with one leg to one side, land on the same side (outside) leg. Then push off as forcefully as possible to the opposite side. Land on the same side leg and repeat in an alternating manner. Be sure that when you push-off you remain low and cover maximum distance. Since speed and distance are both important in lateral jumps, do not sacrifice one quality for the other. (See Figure 2.13, A-F)

   **Note:** To increase the difficulty and to develop even greater explosive power, hold a dumbbell in each hand as you execute the single leg side jumps. Keep the arms flexed and control the weights as you do the jump, so that the dumbbells do not hit the body.

**Figure 2.13: Single leg side jumps**

A        B        C

D        E        F

**CAUTION:**

**1)** Using a slide board may be useful in the early stages of preparation for lateral movement. However, slide boards cannot be used for explosive actions!

**2)** Angled boxes are often used when executing side jumps. However, they are not recommended because the ankle does not experience the same direction of forces as when you execute the cutting action on the ground. In some cases the ankle joint undergoes a completely opposite action. It undergoes eversion rather than inversion. Because of this you do not duplicate what you must do in a game situation and it may lead to ankle sprains.

14. **Barrier side jumps**

**Purpose:** Jumps over objects (barriers) are used to create greater vertical forces in a lateral jump. These are sometimes needed in sports when you must leap over a fallen player or a piece of equipment. These jumps are not recommended for running or lateral movement on a court or field because the objective is usually to stay low for speed and quickness.

**Execution**: Stand with your side to a barrier such as a cone, ball or other object. Leap up and over the object and as soon as you land, fairly close to the object, leap up and back over again. Do not made the jumps very wide. Remain close to the barrier over which you are jumping. This exercise is close to the tuck jump in execution. (See Figure 2.14, A-C)

**Figure 2.14: Barrier side jumps**

A　　　　　　　　　B　　　　　　　　　C

15. **Deep Squat Jumps**

   **Purpose.** This exercise develops power when in a deep squat together with speed of execution. It is most valuable in sports such as weight lifting in which you must go into a squat during execution of the clean. Most often, it is executed with weights held in the hands for greater strength development.

   **Execution.** Assume a standing position with the feet directly under the hips or shoulder width apart. Go into a squat so the thighs are at least parallel to the floor or somewhat deeper if you have the strength and flexibility to execute it through this range of motion. After reaching the lower most position leap up as high as possible with full extension of the legs. Be sure that the legs are straight and the toes are pointed after take off. (See Figure 2.15.1, A-B)

On touchdown, land close to the arch of the foot, i.e. on the ball and then the heel almost simultaneously. As you land, go into the deep squat in one motion and as you reach the lowermost position quickly switch directions and take off as quickly and as powerfully as possible. Prepare yourself mentally and physically for each landing and takeoff.

The "deep" squat jumps can also be done from a 1/2-3/4 squat position if this is the full ROM for the athlete. (See Figure 2.15.2, A-C)

**Figure 2.15.1: Deep Squat Jumps**

A　　　　　　　　　　B

## Figure 2.15.2: Deep Squat Jumps

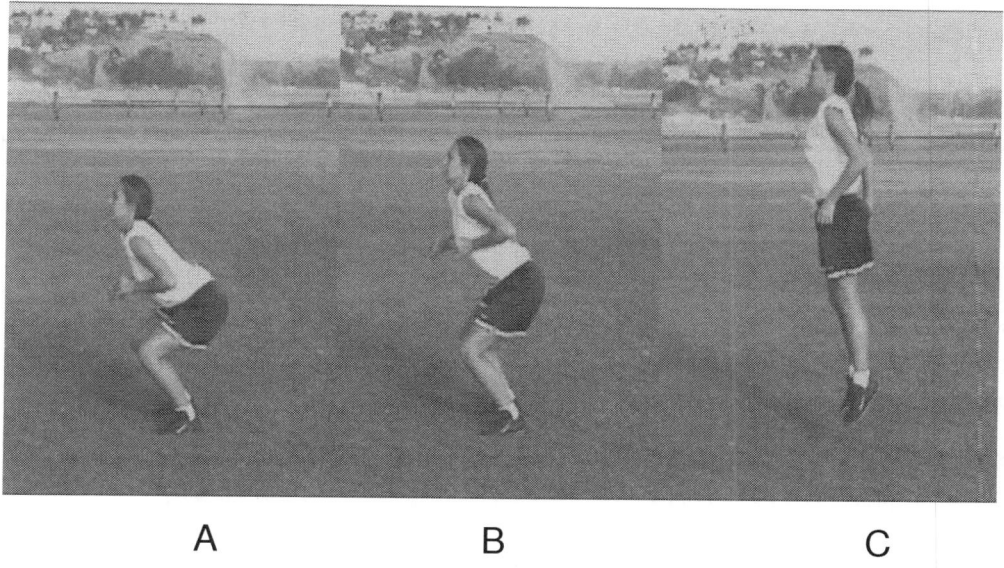

A          B          C

16. **Split Squat Jumps**

    **Purpose.** This exercise is used because you often land, or have to jump, with the feet not directly under the body. This occurs many times in basketball after coming down from a shot or rebound, and in volleyball, soccer, and baseball landings after a jump. The split squat jump develops a quicker and more forceful takeoff. Thus, it is important for open field runners who must make quick changes in direction, especially in forward and backward directions.

    **Execution.** Assume a standing position with your feet under your hips. When you are ready, go into a slight crouch and leap up as high as possible. Once you are airborne, split your legs with one going forward and one going backwards. Hold this position to land in the stride position. Immediately after landing, jump back up and scissor the legs again. Repeat in an alternating manner. The key to successful execution is to leap up as high as possible with full ankle extension and straightening of the legs. Hold a 10-20lb dumbbell in each hand after mastering the exercise without weights. (See Figure 2.16, A-F)

**Figure 2.16: Split Squat Jumps**

A  B  C

D  E  F

## 17. Explosive Leg Press

**Purpose.** To develop a more explosive leg extension, especially in the knee joint. This is an advanced exercise and is not recommended for beginning or intermediate level athletes. You must be physically prepared before attempting this exercise, and you must have a leg press machine that is capable of being used in an explosive manner.

**Execution.** Assume a seated position in an incline leg press machine (preferably at a 45 degree angle or a leg press machine in which you lie flat on your back). Place your feet against the resistance plate squarely in the middle; when you are ready, release the safety catches and lower the resistance plate slightly via leg flexion. When you reach the lowermost point (when the angle of the knee joint is approximately 130-145 degrees) explode with a quick muscular contraction to push the resistance platform away from you. The force generated should be sufficiently great to break contact with the foot. See Figure 2.17.1 A-D.

Before attempting this, be sure that the machine has safety catches that will not allow the resistance platform to fly off the machine. After the resistance platform has moved away from the feet and begins to slide back towards your feet, catch the resistance platform with slightly bent legs to cushion the force but mainly to withstand the force involved and then quickly push the resistance platform back up and away. The faster you "catch" the resistance platform and push it away the more explosive the action.

Before attempting this exercise be sure you have adequate strength and the physical ability to withstand the forces involved when the sled returns and you catch it with the feet. Also, do not attempt to explode maximally when first doing this exercise. Keep pushing harder and harder until you break contact with the resistance platform. Adjust the weights according to your strength capabilities. Start by pushing the platform away only a few inches and get used to catching and then pushing it back as quickly as possible.

Gradually increase the force of the leg extension and the amount of weight being used so that when you push it away, the platform will move approximately the amount that is possible on the machine, and no more. Using too much weight will not allow you to have a strong, explosive contraction. Thus, adjust the weight according to your capabilities for best results.

On some leg press machines, in which you lie flat on your back rather than the resistance platform being in motion, you will find that your body is in motion. Execution is still basically the same so that when you break contact the legs and body move away from the foot platform and then you move in toward the foot plate to cushion and explode back again.

## Figure 2.17.1: Explosive Leg Press

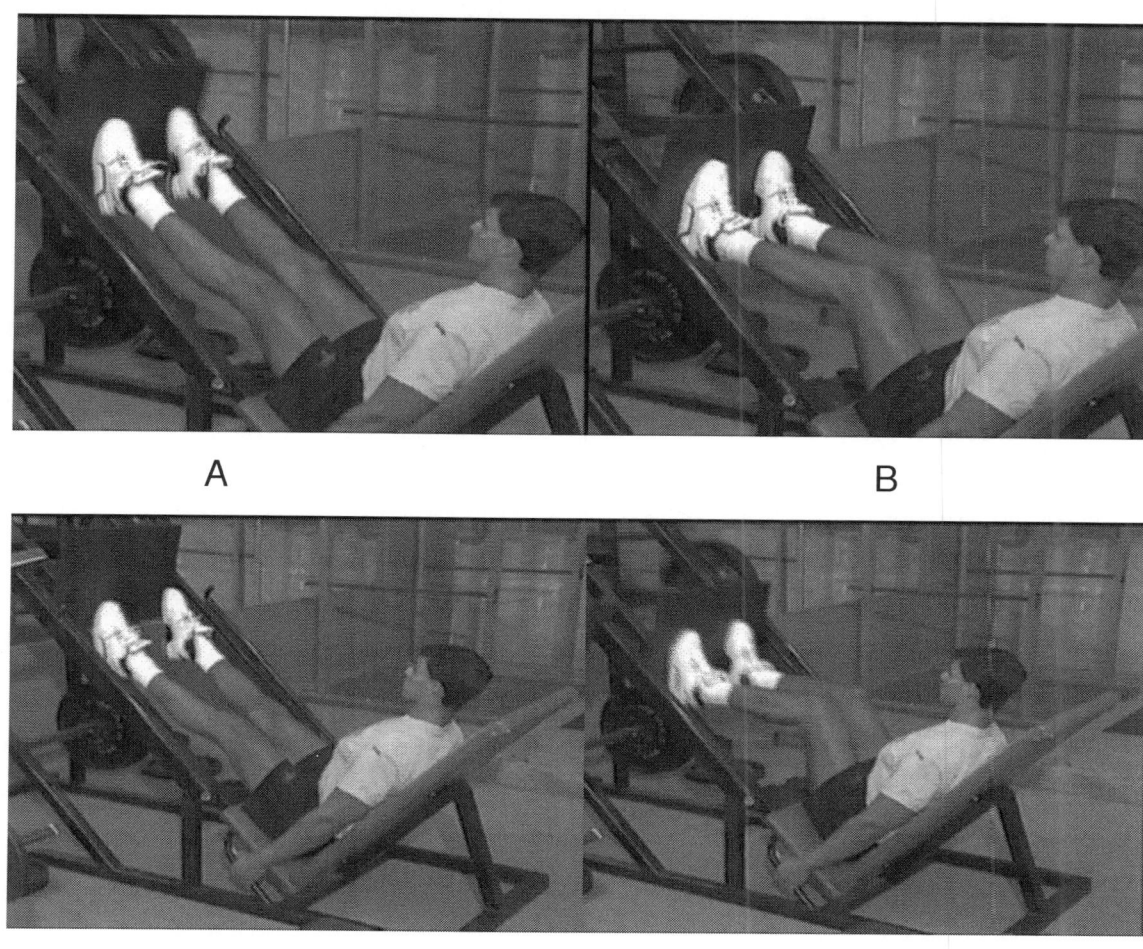

A  B

C  D

For different variants of this exercise see figures 2.17.2, 2.17.3, 2.17.4, and 2.17.5.

**Figure 2.17.2**

Athlete stationary

**Figure 2.17.3**

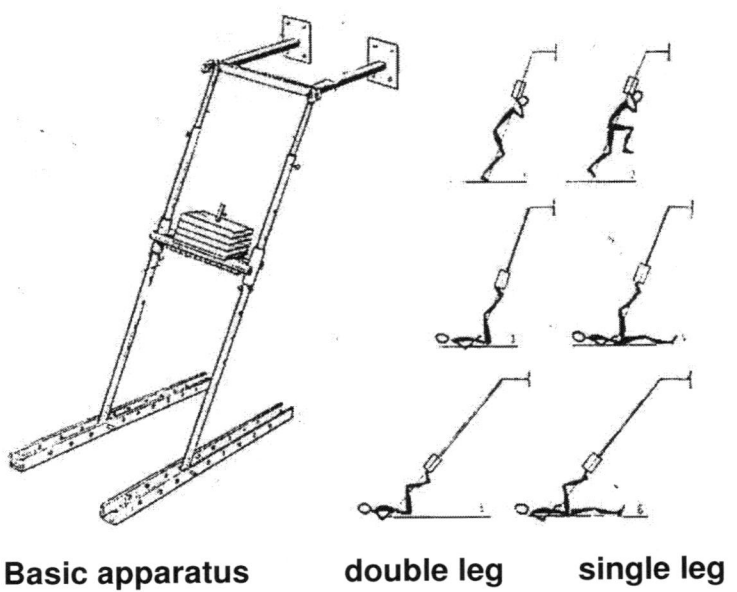

Basic apparatus    double leg    single leg

**Figure 2.17.4**

Athlete moves forward and back

**Figure 2.17.5**

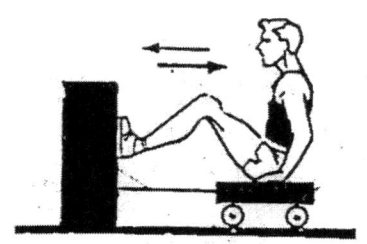

Athlete moves forward and back

## 18. Depth Jump

**Purpose.** Depth jumps improve jump height or more specifically explosive power in the legs. They are also used to improve general quickness, running speed, and cutting actions.

**Execution.** Stand on a raised platform, such as on the first row of bleachers, but, or some other stationary object that is 12 to 30 inches high. When ready, step out with one leg and then drop straight down fairly close to the platform. The key is to drop down in a straight line so there are no forward forces to contend with. Prepare yourself physically and mentally for the landing. Land almost flat-footed, cushion yourself somewhat, and immediately jump up as high as possible, as quickly as possible. Contact and takeoff should take no longer than 0.15 seconds.

Jump straight up after making contact with the ground. Do not execute any other actions after the jump in the initial stages. The key is to concentrate on the landing and takeoff, not on what you will be doing afterwards. (See Figure 2.18, A-F.)

Most important in this exercise is how quickly you execute the landing and takeoff. If you find yourself going very deep, you are probably stepping off from too high a height, or you do not have sufficient eccentric strength to slow you down and stop before leaping upward. In such cases, do additional strength training for eccentric and isometric strength, or lower the height from which you step off.

The height of the jump is important. Very tall or heavy players should not use very high heights. If you are strong and approximately five-six feet tall, you can step off a platform that is approximately 30 inches in height. Do not go any higher. The forces experienced from greater heights create a tendency to sink too low and force you to execute the takeoff slower than what is called for. Also, using higher heights can be disruptive to the CNS even though your may not experience any visible signs of discomfort.

Because of the high-impact forces, very tall players should step off platforms no higher than 24 inches. Very heavy athletes should use a height of 12-15 inches.

At a height of 30 inches, the amount of speed and strength generated in the jump is well balanced and you get the maximum effect of both of these physical qualities. If you increase the height from which you step off, then you must rely more on the strength component and if you lower the height, you will rely more on the speed component. Thus, by adjusting the height of the depth jump you can increase either strength or speed. In general, speed is the most important element needing improvement.

Doing depth jumps two times a week is usually sufficient for most athletes. In some cases, three times per week is acceptable for short periods of time. Also, the number of depth jumps in one session should not be greater than 40 done in sets of 10 reps. For less physically prepared athletes, 20-30 repetitions of the depth jump once a week is sufficient.

Although there is some variability, depth jumps are executed in series (10 times from a lower height and 10 times from slightly higher height). In between each set you should do light running exercises and exercises for relaxation. Because the after-effect of depth jumps is maintained for about 6-8 days, such jumps should be discontinued 1-2 weeks before competition.

### Figure 2.18: Depth Jump

A           B           C

D           E           F

**19. Explosive Knee Drive**

**Purpose.** This exercise duplicates the action of driving the thigh forward which is important for increasing speed, acceleration, stride length, and taking a quick first step.

**Execution.** Attach one end of the Active Cord to a stationary object about knee to mid thigh high and the other end to your ankle. Stand far enough away so there is tension on the tubing when the leg is behind the body. Hold on to a partner or stationary object to stabilize your upper body. Your thigh should be free to move through a full range of motion. Your body should be as erect as possible and the leg to be exercised should be moved behind the body as far as possible to duplicate the thigh position immediately after a push off as seen in running.

When you are ready, inhale slightly more than usual and hold your breath as you bring the leg backward and then forcefully and quickly drive the thigh forward. Your knee should bend so the shin remains basically parallel to the ground as the thigh is driven forward. Drive the thigh forward until it just passes the vertical position. As you return to the initial position under control, quickly reverse directions when to feel a strong stretch on the hip flexor muscles. Repeat for no more than 10 repetitions. Start with five reps to get the feel for the exercise. (See Figure 2.19, A-C)

**Figure 2.19: Explosive Knee Drive**

A                                B                                C

20. **Explosive Lunge**

**Purpose:** This exercise is especially important when you must take a quick, long step as for example when trying to steal a ball, or reaching a ball or for reversing directions. It is also important for increasing your ability to execute an explosive push off as needed not only in reaching for a person or an object, but also for improving running speed and acceleration.

**Execution:** Assume a well-balanced standing position with your feet hip-width apart and the Active Cord non-slip belt around your hips. Inhale and hold your breath as you lean forward and then push the hips forward and forcefully leap out with a long stride, keeping your trunk in a vertical position. Upon landing, your rear leg should be straight but relaxed. You should feel muscle tension in your front leg together with a strong stretch of the hip flexors of the rear leg. After reaching the position, shift your weight and leap backward together with the pull of the cords to return to the original position. (See Figure 2.20, A-C)

Then, to make the lunge even more explosive, quickly push off forward. In essence, you leap, land, and then leap back to the initial position and repeat without any stops. Be sure that you have sufficient tension on the tubing so that you leap against strong resistance and have strong resistance pulling you back. This demands greater eccentric strength on the landing which is used for another explosive forward leap. For variety, rather than having the tubing attached to the D-ring in the middle of the belt in back of your body, you can attach two same tension cords to both sides of the Active Cord belt for greater stabilization of the pelvis.

**Figure 2.20: Explosive Lunge**

A                              B                              C

## 21. Jumping With Cord Resistance

**Purpose:** Attach the non-slip belt around the waist and then attach equal tension cords to both sides of the belt. Attach the other end of the elastic straps to an attachment board or on long stakes driven into the ground approximately 4 feet to either side of the body. There should be tension on the cords in the ready position.

**Execution:** When you are ready, leap up as high as possible and then, as you return downward the cords pull your body down faster. As soon as you make contact with the ground, immediately cushion and explode back upward as quickly as possible. This exercise is executed basically the same way as double leg jumps in place but with the pull of the cords you have greater speed on the down movement of the body, creating greater force on the landing. This enables you to develop even greater force on the return. (See Figure 2.21 for one variant of this exercise.)

## Figure 2.21: Jumping with Cord Resistance

When you become proficient doing this exercise with two cords attached to either side of the body (left-right, or front-back) do the exercise with four equal tension cords attached to the non-slip belt around the waist. In this case, stand in the middle of a rectangle with one cord attached to each corner of the square. The four cords, one on each side of the body are attached to the ring on that side of the body. Be sure to use the same tension cords at each attachment. Execute in the same manner as with the two cords but keep in mind that because you have greater tension on the cords, you will be pulled down even faster so that your contact on the ground will create even more force against which you will have to work.

## 22. Four way single leg jumps

**Purpose:** To develop the ability to jump in any direction off one leg. Very often you may be found in a game situation where you are on your nondominant leg or on a leg from which you do not usually execute a cutting or jumping action. Doing four way single leg jumps prepares you for these jumps.

**Execution**: Assume a standing position on one leg with the other leg bent and off the ground. When ready, inhale and hold your breath as you leap to one side, land and then immediately leap back to the original spot from which you then leap in another direction. You can jump "around the clock" or in a pre-determined manner. (See Figure 2.22 A-D)

The key here is to jump as quickly and as forcefully as possible in the chosen direction. The jumps should be executed for distance, but not so far that they slow you down in the takeoff. Maintaining explosive power is more important than how far you jump on each jump. You must prepare the ankle and a leg for the actions. After doing a set of jumps on one leg switch and repeat on the other leg.

**Figure 2.22: Four way single leg jumps**

A          B          C          D

**Note:** From position D you can then jump in any other direction, i.e., back to the original spot, forward or backward.

There are many jump exercises for the legs. If you use your creativity you will be able to come up with new and interesting exercises. To give you some ideas following are a few slightly different exercises.

**Example 1**

**Example 2**

**Example 3**

**Example 4**

# CHAPTER 3

# EXPLOSIVE ARM TRAINING

Explosive arm actions are very important in sports skills that require a pushing motion where several joint actions occur at the same time but yet in sequence. Examples of this include the shot put, reaching for a ball in basketball, volleyball, tennis, the chest pass in basketball, repelling an opponent in football, and throwing a straight jab in boxing.

Before doing plyometric exercises to develop explosive arms, it is important that you have an adequate strength base and skill-specific strength from doing specialized strength exercises that duplicate the key arm actions. In general, the greater the dynamic correspondence (specific strength) the greater the potential for developing explosive arms. This means that the plyometric exercise must duplicate the action seen in execution of the skill in competitive play.

In strength training, you should emphasize eccentric work, especially exercises in which you "drop and hold". This type of exercise is a takeoff on altitude jumps in which you jump down from a height, undergo slight cushioning, and then hold the position for up to five to six seconds. One such popular exercise is the push-up drop and hold. From a push-up position you push off into the air and then when you land, hold the position after as little cushioning as possible. This concept can be applied to almost every exercise.

All arm plyometric exercises should be done on a resilient surface to prevent injury. Landing on the hands on a hard surface can be injurious to the wrist, especially if you lack finger and wrist strength and flexibility. Because the arms are relatively weaker than the legs, the use of additional resistance - to body weight - is not always needed when doing plyometric arm exercises.

## Active Stretches

Before doing plyometric exercises, it is important that you have an adequate warm-up. The muscles must be ready for the vigorous activity involved. Because of this, you should do active stretches to stimulate and prepare the muscles that will be involved in the exercises. Active stretches not only stretch the muscles and tissues, but prepare the muscles for action.

Do not do slow, static stretches in which you hold a stretch for extended periods of time. They can be detrimental to the joints if held too long, and more importantly, they do not prepare the muscles for action. They figuratively put the muscles to sleep and you will not be able to perform as well as you can.

Some of the best active stretches for the arms and shoulder joints are:

1. *Lateral Arm Raises* (full range of motion overhead)
2. *Front Arm Raises* (full range of motion overhead)
3. *Protraction-Retraction*
4. *Arm Circles* (forward and backward)
5. *Shrugs* (arms alongside the body and overhead)

## *ARM JUMP EXERCISES*

1. **Push-Up Jumps**

    **Purpose:** To develop explosive arms for hitting, throwing, punching and pushing away an opponent.

**Execution:** Assume a push-up position with the body straight from head to toe and with the arms straight and directly under the shoulders. Keep the body rigid, bend the arms, and then push-off to leap up as high as possible. Land on the fingers and then immediately on the whole hand with a little bit of give in the wrist and elbow to cushion the forces. The key is to withstand most of the force and then use the accumulated energy to jump again. Repeat as quickly as possible. Execute on a resilient surface and be sure to flick (flex) the wrists as you end the push-off. See figure 3.1 A-D.

**Figure 3.1: Push-Up Jumps**

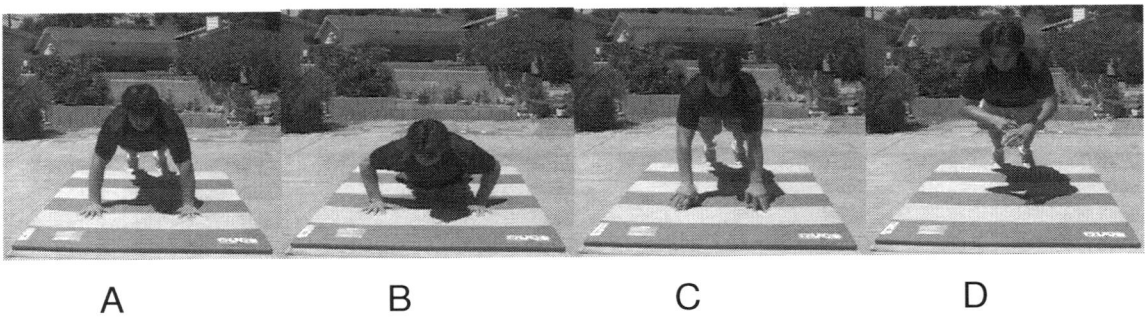

A    B    C    D

When you are proficient in this exercise, do arm jumps over different objects while the feet remain stationary. If he can be on the floor or up on a sturdy box.

2. **Push-Up Jumps with a Clap**

   **Purpose:** Same as push-up jumps.

   **Execution:** Execution is exactly the same as above, but after you are airborne, clap the hands one or more times before landing. In the landing, do not let the chest come close to or touch the floor. Each landing should have some cushioning, but you must be strong enough to withstand the forces on landing with minimum arm bending. If the chest comes close to the floor, work on developing greater eccentric arm and chest strength. See figure 3.2. A-D

**Figure 3.2: Push-Up Jumps with a Clap**

A  B  C  D

3. **Push-Up Jumps with Forward Movement**

   **Purpose:** Same as push-up jumps. In addition, this exercise develops the ability to push off in a slightly different direction.

   **Execution:** Execution is basically the same as in the above exercises. After you flex the arms slightly, push off as you lean the upper body forward so that you travel forward in the jump.

Distance should not be great, a few inches at a time. After you master the exercise, do two, three, or more jumps in a row. If your shoes do not slide easily, do the exercise in your socks. See Figure 3.3 A-H

**Figure 3.3: Push-Up Jumps with Forward Movement**

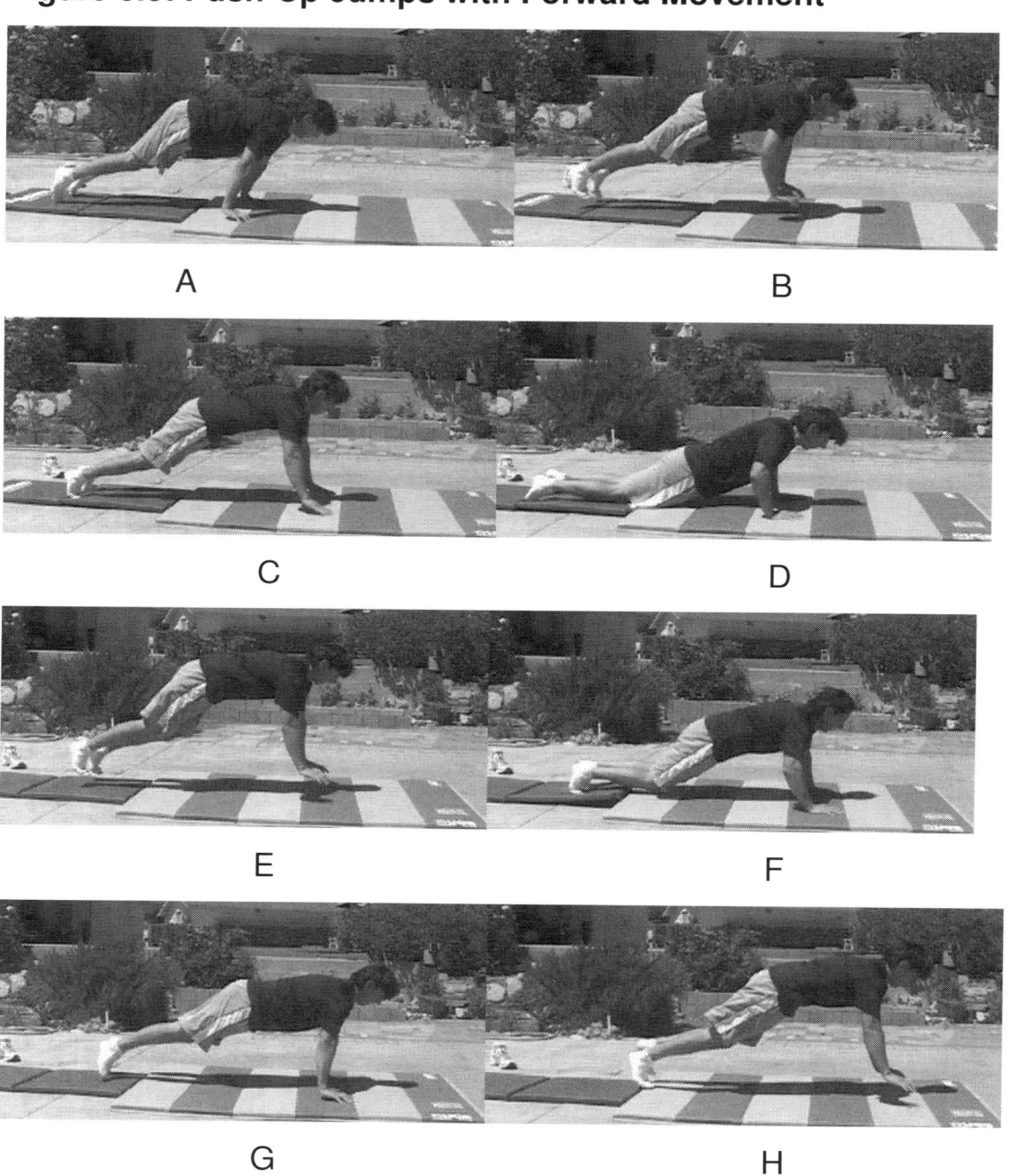

4. **Push-Up Jumps with Backward Movement**

**Purpose:** Same as above, only the push-off is directed backwards.

**Execution:** Execution is the same as above, but instead of pushing off with your weight moving upward and forward, push-off so that as you rise up, you move backward. In essence, you slide to the rear, feet first, a few inches at a time. The use of socks instead of shoes is usually needed. See Figure 3.4 A-H.

## Figure 3.4: Push-Up Jumps with Backward Movement

5. **Single Arm Side Jumps**

   **Purpose:** This is a more advanced exercise that is used to develop the ability to explode with one arm in a sideward direction. It is analogous to single leg side jumps.

   **Execution:** Assume a push-up position with the arms somewhat wider than shoulder distance apart. Arms should be straight in the initial position. When ready, bend one arm slightly and then push off vigorously in the opposite side. At the same time, lift the other arm and prepare to land further out to the same side. As soon as you land, cushion the landing slightly but withstand most of the sideward and downward forces and then push back to the opposite side. Repeat in an alternating manner. This is a difficult exercise and requires ample arm strength. See Figure 3.5 A-I.

### Figure 3.5: Single Arm Side Jumps

6. **Arm Depth Jumps**

   **Purpose:** For maximum loading of the muscles for greater arm quickness. Also for developing arm resiliency and explosive power in forward arm actions.

   **Execution:** Place two sturdy boxes or platforms, slightly wider than shoulder width apart on a resilient mat. Assume a push-up position on the boxes, with the feet in contact with the floor. Hands should be on the top inside edge of the boxes. Bend the arms, leap up and then land on the floor in between the boxes. Cushion the landing forces by bending the arms slightly, and then quickly explode and leap up to the top of the boxes. Pause momentarily, and repeat. When capable, do 5-10 repetitions in a row. See Figure 3.6 A-I

**Figure 3.6: Arm Depth Jumps**

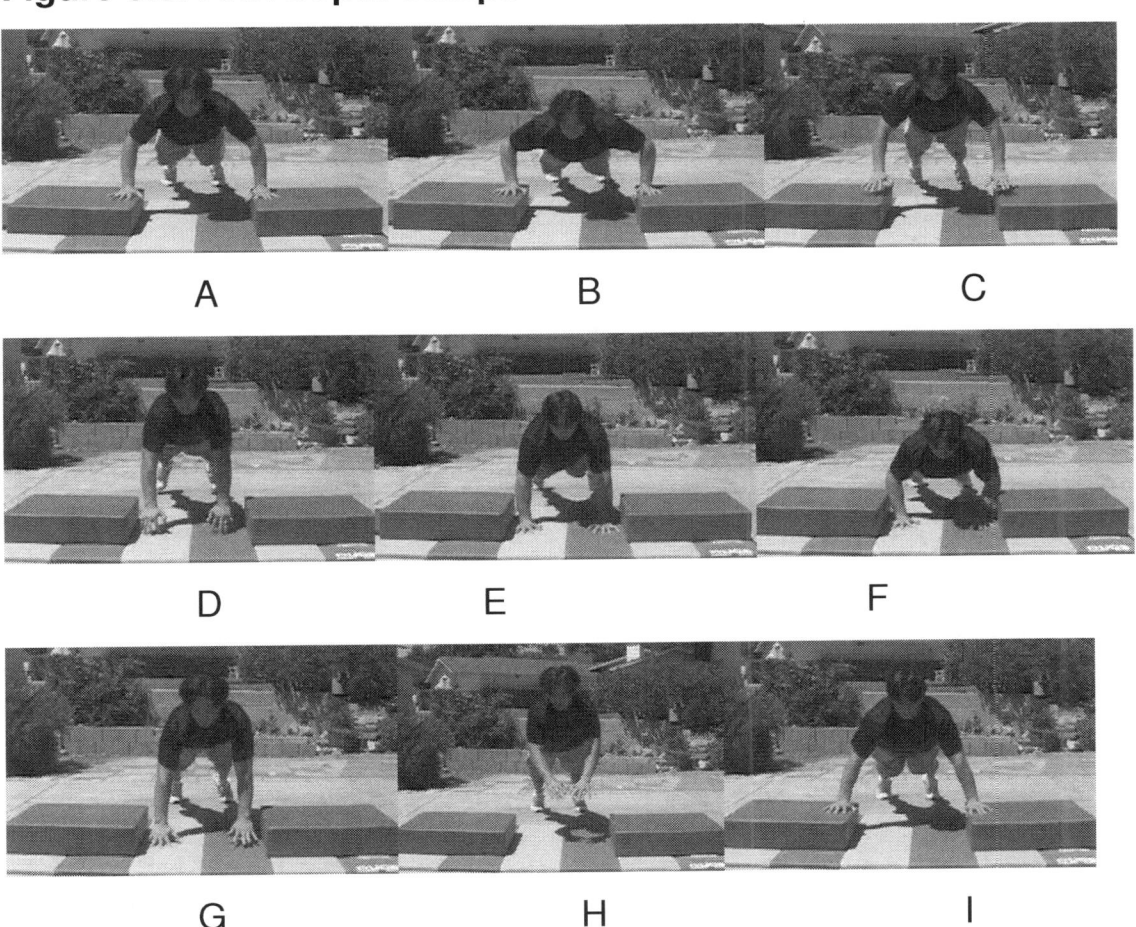

## 7. Handstand Jumps

**Purpose:** To develop explosive arms in overhead actions. These are needed for tackling in football, passing in volleyball, blocking in basketball, tossing a ball upward and for arm jumping as in gymnastics when in a handstand position or in vaulting when pushing off a horse.

**Execution:** Assume a handstand position with the arms straight and directly under the shoulders. If you have difficulty holding the handstand position, do the exercise with the feet against a wall, or have someone hold the legs so that you remain in a vertical position.

Keep the body rigid, bend the arms, and then push off to leap up a few inches above the support surface. Land on the fingers followed immediately by the whole hand, with a little bit of give in the wrist, elbow and shoulder to cushion the forces somewhat. The key is to withstand most of the force and then use the accumulated energy to jump up again. Repeat as quickly as possible. Execute on a resilient surface and be sure to flick (flex) the wrist as you end the push-off when accustomed to the exercise leap up as high as possible. See Figure 3.7 A-F

**Figure 3.7: Handstand Jumps**

A   B   C

D   E   F

8. **Handstand Depth Jumps**

**Purpose:** For maximum loading of the muscles for greater quickness and for developing greater muscle resiliency and explosive power in overhead actions. Do this exercise only after you have mastered the handstand jumps.

**Execution:** Place two sturdy boxes no higher than 6-8 inches, slightly wider than shoulder-width apart on a resilient mat. Assume a handstand position on the boxes with the feet up against a wall or held by a partner. Your hands should be on the top inside edge of the boxes. Bend the arms and then leap up and land on the floor in between the boxes. Cushion the landing forces by bending the arms slightly and then quickly explode and leap up to the top of the boxes. Pause momentarily to prepare yourself for the next repetition. When capable, do 5-10 repetitions in a row. See Figure 3.8 A-H

# Figure 3.8: Handstand Depth Jumps

A	B	C

D	E	F

G	H

## 9. Explosive Bench Press with Dynamic Isometrics

**Purpose:** To develop greater holding and explosive power in the arms. This is needed when pushing (hitting) or holding off an opponent, as in football, boxing, martial arts and free exercise.

**Execution:** Assume a back lying position on a bench holding a barbell on extended arms directly above the upper chest. Lower the bar until it is about halfway to the chest or somewhat less. Then as soon as you begin to push the barbell back up, have two assistants push down on each end of the bar so that you cannot move it. Push hard against the barbell for up to 4-5 sec. at which time the assistants release their hold and you explode and push the barbell upward. The force you generate should be sufficient to quickly straighten the arms.

However, if you exert a greater amount of force the barbell may leave the hands, but should not travel very high because of the weight used. (Approximately 70-75 % of your maximum bench press weight.) If the barbell leaves your hands, be ready to catch it again and have the two assistants also ready to catch the barbell if needed to keep the exercise safe. When you have become proficient in this exercise, you should be able to catch the barbell and handle it on your own.

***Note:*** *This concept can also be applied to other exercises.*

*However, be sure that you are prepared for the intensity that you will experience when using dynamic isometrics in conjunction with an explosive contraction and maximum eccentric loading when receiving or landing as in a jump down.*

**Figure 3.9: Explosive Bench Press with Dynamic Isometrics**

A                                              B

C                                              D

## 10. Explosive Bench Press

**Purpose:** To develop greater holding and explosive power in the arms. This is needed when pushing (hitting) or holding off an opponent, as in football, boxing, martial arts and free exercise.

**Execution:** Assume the usual bench press position holding a barbell with about 50% of your maximum weight, on extended arms above the chest. When ready, inhale and hold your breath as you lower the barbell about halfway to the chest. Then quickly reverse directions and push the barbell back up as quickly and as forcefully as possible. If you use maximum force the barbell should be accelerated to such an extent that it will leave your hands as you release it. However the weight that you are using should not allow the barbell to travel very high -- usually about four to 6 inches.

Quickly exhale and then inhale and hold your breath in preparation for receiving the barbell on extended arms. As contact is made allow the extended arms to flex to absorb some of the catching forces but mainly to withstand and accumulate the forces. When sufficient force is generated, quickly reverse directions and blast the barbell back up and release it once again. Repeat for up to five repetitions if you are executing the exercise under control and with good form. See Figure 3.10.

**Figure 3.10: Explosive Bench Press**

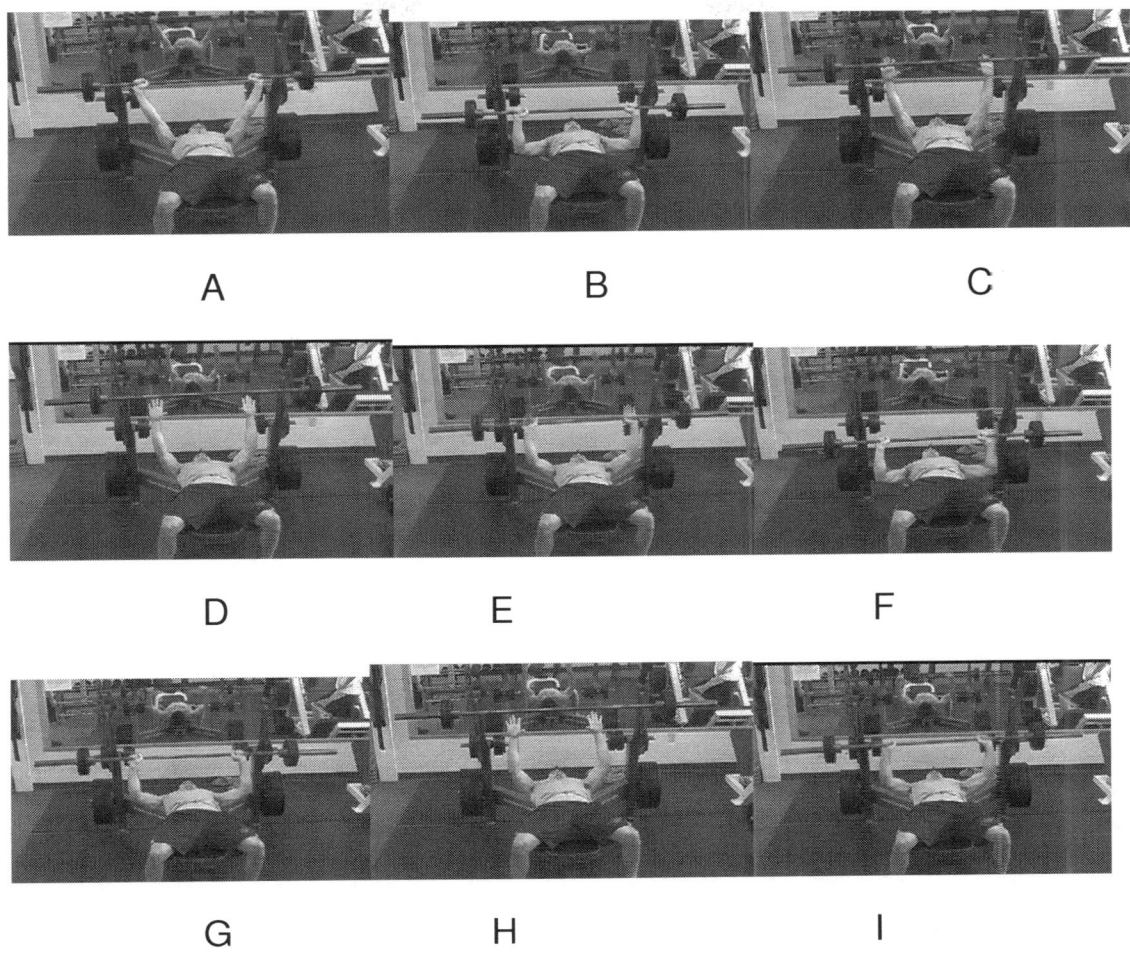

11. **Chest Pass**

**Purpose:** To develop explosive arms as used in ball passing and pushing actions. This exercise is similar to the explosive bench press but uses medicine balls and a partner. It is more specific to most sports actions. In general, this exercise is used most often with youngsters and novices who are not ready to handle the explosive bench press. However, when executed explosively is also a great exercise for higher-level athletes.

**Execution:** Assume a square stance facing a partner approximately 10 feet away. Hold a medicine ball in two hands chest high so that the thumbs face the body and the little fingers point to the opposite side. Push-throw the ball so that it can be caught chest high by your partner. Your partner receives the ball and quickly pushes it back to you. You then catch it and quickly throw the ball back to your partner. Pronate the hands as you throw the ball (palms face out to the sides and the fingers point forward after release). Execute the catch and push as quickly as possible. To ensure quickness, do not use very heavy balls. See figure 3.11.

**Figure 3.11: Chest Pass**

A        B        C

D        E        F

## 12. Explosive Chest Pass

**Purpose:** Same as in exercise 11 but to develop quicker and faster acting arms. This exercise can be used with athletes on all levels but especially the high-level.

**Execution:** Hold the handles of two equal tension Active cords in the hands chest high. Move away from the stationary attachment until you have ample tension on the cords. When ready, inhale and hold your breath as you quickly straighten the arms out straight in front of you. The action is basically the same as in a medicine ball pass, in a boxing jab punch, etc., but executed as rapidly as possible for five to six repetitions. The resistance on the cords should not be too light as it can injure the elbows when performed as quickly as possible. But it should also not be too great so that the arm extension is slowed down. This is a great exercise for sports that require quick repetitive actions. See figure 3.12 A-F.

### Figure 3.12: Explosive Chest Pass

### 13. Wrist Break Using Ulna Flexion

**Purpose:** To develop a quicker wrist break which is needed in many throws and hits, especially in the golf and baseball swings and lacrosse pass.

**Execution:** Stand holding a Strength bar in one hand with the weighted end pointed to the rear. Start with the bar slightly above level (wrist ulna flexed) and then lower it until it is slightly below level. As you reach the end position quickly reverse directions. Pause in between each rep or do five-six repetitions in a row with no stopping. On the last repetition bring the bar up as high as possible with the arm fully extended. Then stop, relax, and place the bar in the other hand and repeat. The key in this exercise is to have quick reversals of direction in the bottom position.

See Figure 3.13 A-F.

**Figure 3.13: Wrist Break Using Ulna Flexion**

A      B      C

D      E      F

## 14. Single Arm Catch-Pushes

**Purpose:** To use one arm in an explosive manner. For use in sports such as the shot-put, football stiff-arming, boxing, and sports requiring quick arms for reaching a ball (tennis, basketball, volleyball, lacrosse, etc.)

**Execution:** Construct a pendulum type apparatus and hang a medicine ball or some other weight at the bottom end, similar to a grandfather clock (See Figure 3.14.1). Stand alongside the pendulum when it is stationary and adjust the ball (weighted end) so that is at the height at which you wish to receive it, (usually at approximately shoulder height). Push the ball away and as it comes back, "catch" the ball with the hand. Bend the arm to partially absorb but mainly to withstand the forces received at impact and then push the ball away explosively, i.e., as quickly and as forcefully as possible. The further you push the ball away the more force it will have as it comes back at you. See Figure 3.14.2 for a variant.

Similar devices can be used to produce similar effects. For example, rails or dollies upon which an object (or you) can slide down to receive and repel with one or both arms. Also useful are different forms of slides where a ball comes at you for receiving and "throwing" back. See Figure 3.14.3 for an example.

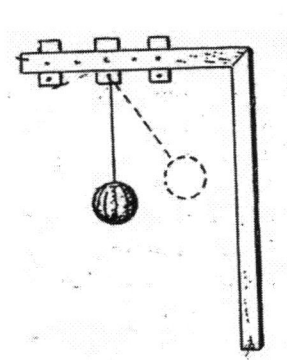

**Figure 3.14.1**

**Figure 3.14.2**

**Figure 3.14.3**

15. **T-Bench Explosive Medial Rotation with Wrist Flick**

**Purpose:** This exercise is very important to develop the shoulder joint medial rotator muscles which are used in all throwing actions, and in many overhead hitting actions. It can be combined with the wrist flick.

**Execution:** Place two exercise benches against one another so that the long axis of one bench is perpendicular to the long axis of the other bench. In their final position the benches should form the letter "T." Assume a back lying position on the long bench so that when you are lying on your back your shoulders will be at the far edge of the cross bench in line with your arm(s) which should also be on the far edge of the bench. Hold the forearm up so that it is 90 degrees to the upper arm. Lower the forearm to the rear while maintaining the right angle in the elbow joint until the forearm is approximately 45 degrees to the vertical.

Your partner should hold a small ball in front, directly above you about 12-15 inches away. He then drops the ball so that you can catch it, bring the forearm back in shoulder joint lateral rotation and then quickly rotate the arm to bring the forearm up and then flick the wrist to complete the throw. Concentrate mainly on bringing the forearm up prior to flicking the wrist at the end. Repeat once you resume the initial position. See figure 3.15, A-C.

Be sure you have sufficient strength of the muscles involved before doing the explosive version. Do not use too heavy a ball. Usually two to five pounds is more than enough. Using too much weight or too high a height can put great stress on the shoulder and should be avoided.

**Figure 3.15: T-Bench Explosive Medial Rotation with Wrist Flick**

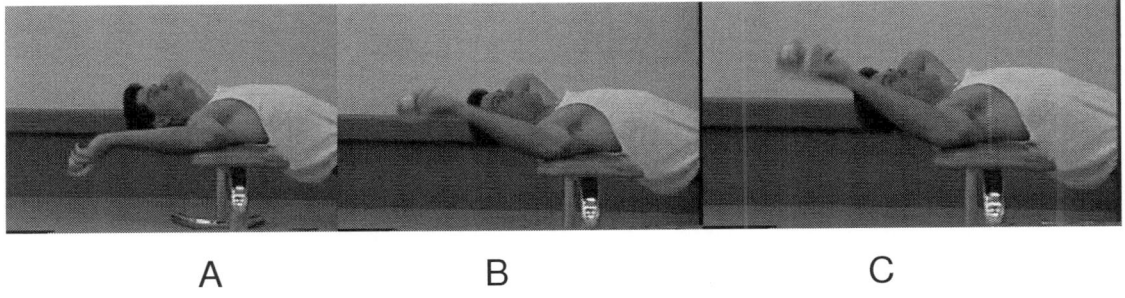

A　　　　　　　　B　　　　　　　　C

# CHAPTER 4

# EXPLOSIVE MID-SECTION TRAINING

Mid-section explosive plyometric training is perhaps the most overlooked area in the training of athletes. This is unfortunate since execution of most sports skills that require power use hip and shoulder rotation. In the throwing and hitting skills, hip and shoulder rotation actions contribute over one third of the total force generated. In some cases it can reach 50% and more!

An explosive mid-section is needed in sports such as football (passing, cutting, blocking, tackling), baseball, softball (pitching, throwing from the outfield, batting), basketball (mainly for cutting), field events (javelin, shot, discus), golf, tennis (and other racket sports), boxing, the martial arts, lacrosse and hockey (shooting and cutting). In kicking, hip and shoulder rotation play an important role in bringing and maintaining the thigh in correct position to execute the kick.

Rotation of the hips but especially the shoulders, moves the greatest amount of body mass that, when accelerated, quickly produces great force. When you get the hip and shoulder actions executed before the arms go into action, the arms will be in motion without actually using muscles that move the arm. Also, the arm will get "cocked" ready for more force producing in the throw or hit from the shoulder rotation.

Many shoulder and elbow problems are created when you rely mostly on the arm for power in a throwing action. But if you first get the hips and shoulders involved, the arm action will be able to contribute even more force, without stress and will feel easier. Let the body (legs, hips and shoulders) generate most of the force and use the arms more for accuracy of the hit or throw, while still contributing force.

For example, a professional baseball player with whom I worked wanted improvement in his throwing. When I did a visual biomechanical analysis of his throwing (which he thought was good),

I found that the throw was executed basically with his legs and arm. After striding he threw mainly with the arm. By working on sequencing the hip and shoulder rotation he developed more effective technique, and was amazed at the difference in his throws. According to him, "My throws are now effortless and going faster than ever before."

You can experience great improvement by coupling technique with strength and explosive exercises (specialized exercises -- conjugate method) to develop more strength and explosive power. To prepare yourself for the plyometric exercises first do strength exercises such as the reverse trunk twist, back raise, back raise with a twist, Russian twist and sit-ups on the Yessis Back Machine (Glute-Ham Developer.) Once a strength base is developed, doing plyometric rotational exercises will produce dramatic results in your throwing, hitting and other skills.

## Active Stretches

Before doing explosive exercises, it is important that you have an adequate warm-up. The muscles must be ready for the vigorous activity involved. Because of this, you should do active stretches to stimulate and prepare the muscles that will be involved in the exercises. Active stretches not only stretch the muscles and tissues but prepare the muscles for the action by activating and warming them up. Do not do slow, static stretches in which you hold a stretch for extended periods of time.

Some of the best active stretches for the midsection are:

1. *Good Morning (Hamstring Stretch)*
2. *Standing Side Stretch (Side Bend)*
3. *Hip and Side Stretch (Side Bend with shifting of the hips)*
4. *Standing Twist (shoulders only)*
5. *Shoulder and Hip Rotation (Full standing Twist)*
6. *Reverse Trunk Twist*
7. *Forward and backward bends*

## *PLYOMETRIC EXERCISES*

1. **Lateral Hip Drive (Lateral weight shift)**

   **Purpose**: To learn the feel and action involved in driving the hips forward as typically needed in throwing and hitting actions and to develop strength of the hip muscles involved in the hip drive. This is not a plyometric exercise although it is a precursor to doing the true plyometric version. It is needed before you can safely do the mid-section plyometric exercises.

**Execution:** Attach an Active Cord to the non-slip belt around the hips and stand sideways to the fixed attachment at the other end. The attachment should be hip high and the cord have strong tension. Stand in a side facing position the same as you do when executing a specific throw or hit. Inhale and push the hips back an inch or so and then quickly shift the hips forward (sideways) over the front leg which is furthest from the cord attachment. Keep the hips level during the push so that the action is isolated to the rear hip joint. Your head and shoulders may shift forward a little and this is acceptable but keep your trunk erect at all times. Exhale as you return to the initial position, relax and then repeat. See figure 4.1.1

To make execution more specific to sports in which you stride forward, (for example, baseball pitching and batting, throws from the outfield), do the exercise with a forward step immediately after you get the hips moving forward. In other words, initiate the exercise in exactly the same manner by pushing the hips forward. As your weight is shifting forward, step out with the forward leg to increase the distance over which your weight is shifted and to regain your balance. This movement is analogous to doing a side lunge. See Figure 4.1.2

To make the exercise explosive, as needed in sports that require quickness, leap sideways as you strongly and quickly push the hips forward (sideways) after the reverse switch. Leap forward and back as quickly as possible for up to five to six repetitions. As you become more proficient work up to 10 repetitions for one or more sets. See Figure 4.1.3.

This exercise can be done in place so that the push off leg remains stationary and you in essence leap off the one leg. It can also be done with a leaping action in which the push off leg leaves the ground and advances forward. After landing in the new position, you can pause and hold in the landing position and leap back and repeat quickly. For variety, you can also execute one or two repetitions and then relax before you repeat.

## Figure 4.1.1: Lateral Hip Drive

A                                                          B

## Figure 4.1.2:  Side lunge

A                              B                              C

**Figure 4.1.3: Explosive Side Lunge**

A            B            C

D            E            F

2. **Front facing hip and shoulder rotation throws**

   **Purpose:** To develop the ability to explosively rotate the hips and mainly the shoulders, as needed in quick throwing for short distances, quick passes in hockey and especially in reactive hitting, baseball hitting and other skills.

   **Execution:** Assume a front facing position to a partner standing approximately 10-15 feet away. Hold a medicine ball in your hands and then rotate the shoulders (trunk) back 90 degrees to bring the ball out to the side and back. From this position, rotate the shoulders forward and release the ball. Keep the arms in the same position with the shoulders so that when you release the ball it is from the shoulder rotation, not from swinging the arms forward. See figure 4.2 A-F.

If there is sufficient time emphasized the hip rotation prior to the shoulder rotation. They should be done in very quick sequential actions. These actions must be mastered if you wish to generate maximum force in your throws and hits.

**Figure 4.2: Front facing hip and shoulder rotation throws**

A　　　　　　　　B　　　　　　　　C

D　　　　　　　　E　　　　　　　　F

3. **Side facing throws**

   **Purpose:** To develop the ability to explosively rotate the hips and shoulders but mainly the shoulders.

   **Execution:** Stand sideways to your partner, approximately 10-15 feet away. The same side arm should be facing the inside. Hold a ball on outstretched arms, bring the ball back with only hip and shoulder rotation and then rotate forward, beginning with the hips followed by the shoulders. The ball should reach your partner in front of the body so that he can grasp it on extended arms and quickly return it to you. Speed of execution especially in the catch-throw, is most important in this exercise. Because of this limit your rotational movements to the rear or forward. Isolate the action to hip and shoulder rotation in sequence or to mainly shoulder rotation.

**Figure 4.3: Side facing throws**

## 4. Forward overhead throws

**Purpose:** To use the trunk in a forward throwing action. This requires strong abdominals and ample forward-backward flexibility in the midsection. It is needed in overhead hitting and throwing actions such as in a volleyball spike, tennis serve and, to a good extent, in baseball pitching, the javelin throw and soccer throw-in.

**Execution:** Stand close to a partner in a front facing position. Hold a medicine ball on extended arms completely over the head. Arms should remain straight or as straight as possible during the execution. Lean back with the shoulders and trunk to place the abdominals on stretch and then, keeping the arms in the same alignment with the shoulders, contract the abdominals to pull the trunk forward to release the ball.

Your partner should catch the ball up high on extended arms, and then cushion the ball slightly by arching the back to the rear. This places the abdominals on stretch so that they can then contract and bring the shoulders (upper body) forward to release the ball.

This is a difficult exercise to coordinate and master on the throws. However, once learned it is a very effective exercise. The key is to not use the arms for the throwing action. Use the movement of the upper body forward by contraction of the abdominals to throw the ball.

**Figure 4.4: Forward overhead throws**

# CHAPTER 5

# TOTAL BODY EXPLOSIVE TRAINING

Execution of most basic and sports skills, involve the whole body. In some of the basic skills such as running, jumping and kicking, the amount of force developed by the different body parts is substantially different than in throwing and hitting.

In throwing and hitting skills, the legs, midsection and arms can each contribute up to one-third of the total force produced. By putting greater emphasis on either the legs, midsection or arms, the ratios can change. Ideally, using the entire body is more efficient and safer than relying on only one or two areas for the production of most force. The only exceptions are when there is insufficient time to use the whole body. This often occurs in sports such as tennis (volleys), baseball (quick infield throws), hockey quick shots and passes and short quick bullet passes in football.

The key to successful utilization of the entire body is in the integration of each body part into a smooth sequential pattern. This is where total body explosive training can play an important role. In the previous chapters you learned how to mainly execute individual plyometric exercises for the legs, mid-section and arms. Covered in this chapter is integration of these three body areas with some variations in the amount of force applied by the body parts.

To make an exercise as specific as possible to your sport, emphasize those actions that are used to a greater extent for successful execution of the skill. For example, in the exercises that do not require trunk rotation, stabilize the trunk so that the force from the legs can be transferred to the arms.

## Active Stretches

Before doing explosive exercises, it is important that you have an adequate warm-up. The muscles must be ready for the vigorous activity involved. Because of this, you should do active stretches to stimulate and prepare the muscles that will be involved in the exercises. Active stretches not only stretch the muscles and tissues but prepare the muscles for the action by activating and warming them up. Do not do slow, static stretches in which you hold a stretch for extended periods of time.

There are no special active stretches that can be recommended for the entire body. Select one or two lower body, one or two midsection and a few upper body exercises depending upon your needs and the exercise you are about to do. The key is to prepare your body for the intense activity; never start "cold," as this leads to injury.

## *TOTAL BODY EXPLOSIVE EXERCISES*

1. **Jump Out Of Squat with Ball Toss Upward**

    **Purpose:** To coordinate leg, trunk and arm movements in a jumping-throwing pattern.

**Execution:** Assume a semi-squat position holding a ball on extended arms between the legs. When ready, dip down to quickly tense the muscles then leap up and slightly forward as fast as possible. Release the ball upward at the height of the jump, landing slightly in front of the take off spot. Do not leap very far forward; emphasis should be on an upward jump and throw.

**Figure 5.1: Jump Out Of Squat with Ball Toss Upward**

A          B          C

2. **Jump with a Forward Throw from a Side Facing Position**

   **Purpose:** To coordinate leg, trunk rotation and arm movements in a jumping/throwing pattern.

   **Execution:** Execution is basically the same as in Figure 5.1 except that you begin in a side facing position to the target. For example, for a right-handed person, stand with the left side of the body facing the target and assume a semi-squat position holding the ball just outside the right leg. When ready, bring the ball up, then jump up and rotate the shoulders forward (to the left) to complete the throw to the target.

Begin slowly and gradually increase the force of the jump and throw. Depending upon your sport, the throw can be directed more in a forward or upward direction. Do this exercise throwing from both sides to have balanced development and to increase your ability on one or both sides See Figure 5.2.1. A good prerequisite strength exercise to duplicate this movement is the barbell squat with a 90 degree shoulder turn as you rise up -- but do not jump. See Figure 5.2.2.

**Figure 5.2.1:**

**Jump with a Forward Throw From a Side Facing Position**

A          B          C

D          E          F

**Figure 5.2.2: Squat with a 90 degree turn**

3. **Jump Out of Squat with a Chest Pass**

   **Purpose:** To coordinate a jumping action with arm actions, i.e. jumping and passing.

   **Execution:** Assume a standing position holding a medicine ball in both hands on extended arms or up by the chest. When ready, squat down and leap upward as high as possible. Pass the ball when at the peak of the jump, i.e., execute a chest pass. See Figure 5.3

### Figure 5.3: Jump Out of Squat with a Chest Pass

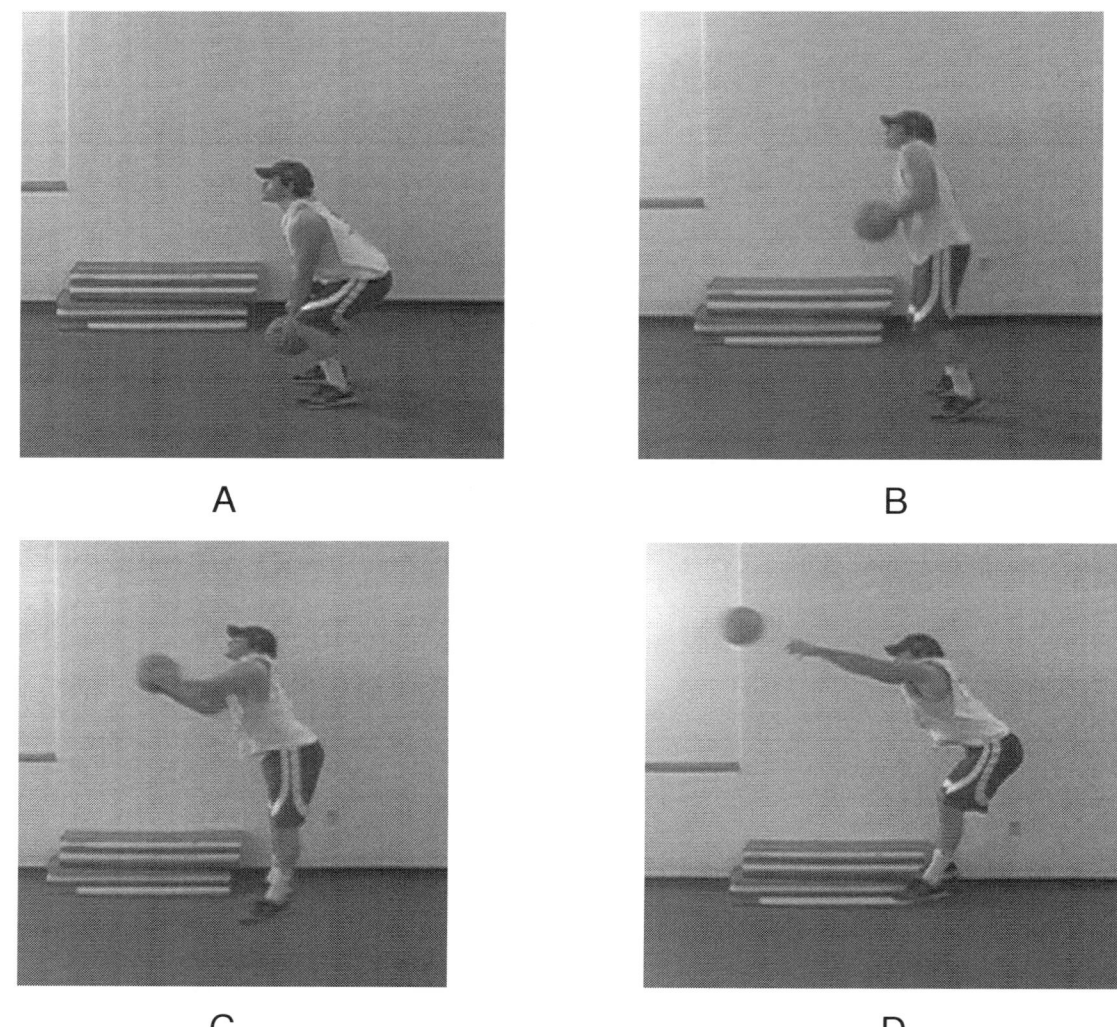

A

B

C

D

### 4. Upward Leap with a Backward Throw

**Purpose:** To coordinate backward arm movements with an upward leap. To develop the ability to go into a back arch position which is so important in many throwing and hitting sports, as for example in the shot, discus and javelin, tennis serve and baseball pitch.

**Execution:** Assume a semi-squat position holding a medicine ball between the legs on extended arms. When ready, fully extend the body, leap upward, and then throw the ball with straight arms over the head as high and as far backwards as possible. Do not bend the arms in execution of the throw; they should remain straight at all times. Use the legs and trunk for production of force, not the arms. Do the standing backward ball toss to prepare yourself for this exercise. Good prerequisite strength exercises are the back raise and glute-ham-gastroc raise.

**Figure 5.4: Upward Leap with a Backward Throw**

A        B        C

# Role of Body Parts

In the above exercises, explosive leg actions are needed to get the body airborne. However, in many sports that involve hitting, as for example, tennis ground strokes but mainly in the golf swing, the feet are in contact with the ground when the stroke or swing is executed. The legs and/or hips participate to start the initial movement to produce weight shift.

Weight shift is important to get the body in motion to create momentum and to then have the forces generated transferred to the midsection (when the hips undergo rotation). This accumulated force is then transferred together with the force produced by the shoulder rotation to the arms when hitting a ball. The same applies to a person throwing a punch in boxing, or throwing a ball as in baseball pitching, or the quarterback passing, or an object such as the javelin, shot and discus.

Because of the need to integrate these movements in proper sequence it is impossible to do plyometric exercises that duplicate all of the body actions that are involved in one exercise. Certain portions can be worked on individually while performing parts of the total skill. This is seen in the following examples:

## Medicine Ball Throws

From a side facing position begin leaning forward (sideways) and then step with the forward leg. Shift and rotate the hips forward after touchdown while holding a ball on extended arms to the rear. After the hips have cleared, rotate the shoulders forward and bring the arms forward to release the ball. The emphasis here is on the abdominal oblique muscles to rotate the shoulders around explosively after the forward stride and hip rotation which pretenses the oblique muscles.

You can also use Active Cords instead of a medicine ball. For example, hold the handle of the cord in the right hand by the right shoulder and hold this position during the shoulder rotation. As you rotate the shoulders to the front facing position, push the hand forward as in a boxing punch (jab). Hold the hand at the level needed; usually around the waist in tennis and baseball hitting, shoulders in boxing, and so on.

A similar exercise can be done for the golf swing. Instead of leaning and striding forward to initiate weight shift, a non-slippable belt as in the Active Cords set is placed around the hips so that you must first drive the hips forward against the resistance of the tubing and then rotate the hips. Follow this action with shoulder rotation and a ball toss in an underhand pattern. This exercise can be adapted to tennis, baseball and other hitting/throwing events, by first leaning and then stepping forward against the resistance of the Active Cord(s).

Other exercises in which the hips are first pulled around by a tensed Active Cord can also be used. This action is then followed by loaded shoulder rotation and arm actions. These exercises are used mainly to enhance hip rotation and develop a feel for the action.

The key to executing such exercises is to have a good understanding of the sequence of actions involved in execution of the main skills used in your sport, i.e. technique. With the use of Active Cords and medicine balls you can create exercises to enhance force production in many sports skills. It is also a very effective way of increasing the speed and explosive force generated by any major body part action, whether it is the legs, midsection or arms.

# CHAPTER 6

# INTEGRATION OF EXPLOSIVE PLYOMETRICS

To achieve your maximum potential, you must possess outstanding technique, strength, explosive power and other physical abilities, specific to the actions that you must execute in your sport. Because of this, training time must be spent on coupling technique with the physical qualities, and especially the explosive ones. This is known as specialized strength and explosive training also known as conjugate training and dynamic correspondence. Each method uses a combination of skill technique and the development of a specific physical quality.

Your physical abilities, age and skill proficiency, play very important roles in regard to the type and amount of training that you do. For example, if you are a young high school player who has never weight trained, you will see great improvement in technique and strength from strength training. Higher level athletes need more speed-strength (explosive plyometric) and strength work coupled with technique (specialized exercises). Range of motion, starting strength, reactive abilities and other factors are incorporated into the strength and plyometric training.

Development of only absolute strength can have a negative effect on speed, quickness and explosiveness. But absolute strength increases are needed to develop even more speed and explosiveness. Thus, you should do more exercises in the 75 to 85% of maximum zone rather than 90 to 100% as is usually done in absolute strength training. This lower intensity zone has proven to be the most effective for improving performance. The 90 to 100% zone is best suited for increases to lift heavier weights, which is not the objective for most athletes. In addition, strength training should be complemented with explosive plyometric training so that you do not lose speed.

It is effective to combine two or three training objectives into one training session, especially with high-level athletes, similar to what takes place in block training. However, novice and low-level athletes experience greater gains from complex training involving a multitude of objectives and methods. Not only does this help economize on time, but it leads to greater increases in each physical quality. As a result, you become a better conditioned and trained athlete instead of emphasizing only one kind of training for certain periods. However, the training exercises and methods to be used and how they are grouped or sequenced is determined by the demands of your sport, your athletic preparedness, technique and mastery of game skills.

To better comprehend how integration can be accomplished you must first understand the concept of periodization and cycling. By following the tenants of periodization you can get maximum results from your training and workout routines in the shortest amount of time.

## PERIODIZATION

In periodization, the year is divided into different periods or phases of training. In each phase you train to gain certain physical qualities or results. Another way of saying this is that you attain sports form in the exercises and skills etc. used in that period of training. The development you achieve then enables you to do the training called for in the next period of training. In this way the positive changes you experience from each period of training makes it possible for you to tackle the next phase of training which eventually leads to your ultimate goal. It culminates in getting you ready to compete.

The periodization plan is basically the same for all athletes. There are four periods which can last anywhere from one to six months. They are as follows:

## PHASE I - General Physical Preparation (GPP)

GPP is the initial stage of training. It starts every cycle of training from the macro- meso- and microcycle after restoration and recovery. It consists primarily of general preparatory and some specialized conditioning exercises to work all the major muscles and joints. This preparation prepares you for the more intense training such as explosive plyometrics, which follows. This period is also used for rehabilitation of injured muscles and joints, strengthening or bringing up to par the lagging muscles and improvement of technique. Thus, explosive plyometrics is not used in this period. Simple and easy jump exercises play the major role.

For the high-level and elite athlete, GPP is used more for recovery and warm up rather than for developmental purposes. This is based on the premise that high level and elite athletes maintain their physical condition throughout the year and train throughout the year on a specific periodization scheme. This is a major distinguishing characteristic of the high-level athlete.

The training in GPP is general in nature so that psychological stress does not build up. You accustom the body to working out with many different exercises and activities. The volume of work done is high, but the intensity is low. This period of training must be used by all athletes regardless of sport, to prepare the body for future training. This is especially true of novice and mid-level athletes. All too often however, many athletes especially professional athletes, in baseball and football, do only GPP to prepare for the season. Doing this does not allow them to fully develop their potential and become better each year. It also raises the question whether they are truly elite or high-level.

High level athletes who must compete most of the year must maintain a high level of fitness and readiness to perform on the highest levels. Because of this, the typical periodization scheme does not work for them. They use what is known as the Block Periodization system. In this they go through special mesocycles to prepare themselves for competition.

*Elite athletes are always fit and only specialize for brief periods of time to peak*

After each major competition they basically go through the three phases as in the above described periodization scheme, but not to the same extent. After they have had some time for recovery they then work on only a few or a limited number of physical qualities that are lagging or must be improved for greater success. The work at this time is highly specialized. For more information on block training see *Block Periodization: Breakthrough in Sports Training,* by Dr. Vladimir Issurin. It can be found on the DrYessis.com website.

# PHASE II - Specialized Physical Training (SPP)

This is the main phase of training for speed, power and explosive athletes. The SPP begins gradually as the GPP draws to a close so that there is a general transition from general to specific training. In SPP, the work is very specific to the sport. Almost all the exercises that you use duplicate as closely as possible the actions involved in execution of the key skills involved in competitive play. Because of this these exercises become the backbone of your program.

These specialized exercises are very specific since they must duplicate the technique involved in the sports skill execution. This means duplicating or coming as close as possible to the technique and muscle action involved in the competitive skill. This is why such training is also known as dynamic correspondence since the exercises correspond very closely to the competitive skill. You see an immediate improvement from doing such specialized exercises. But you must be able to demonstrate effective technique.

By doing specialized exercises that include explosive plyometrics and incorporating them into your skill execution and game play, you will see dramatic results – much greater than you will ever see from a general conditioning program. You will be amazed at your performance after such training!

# PHASE III - The Competitive Period

As SPP comes to a close it blends into the competitive period. Near the end of the specialized period many of the exercises and drills duplicate actual competitive situations. In season (during competition), emphasis is on maintaining the physical qualities (speed, strength, etc.) developed in SSP. In many sports such as track, explosive plyometrics continue to be done in order to develop even greater speed and power. In these sports explosive plyometrics also serve for doing specific high-intensity warm-ups and/or to maintain or improve explosive power.

# PHASE IV - The Post Competitive Period

Regardless of your sport, after you compete you should go through a stage of recuperation and relaxation, mainly from a mental standpoint. During the competitive season the psychological stress is usually quite high and you must be able to remove this stress quickly, before the body reacts negatively. At this time the body can still do physical work but the mind must rest. But you should never do explosive plyometrics at this time because the intensity is too great.

Best at this time is active rest, which means that you remain active for relaxation purposes, not for physical development. Very effective is to participate in a different sport that you do well, so you can still experience the physical work, but also get enjoyment and satisfaction from the playing to help you relax.

The post competitive period usually lasts 1-4 weeks. If the competitive period is relatively short as for example, only one week of competition, then only a few days of the post competitive period is needed. However, if you have a long season lasting 4-5 months, then you should take at least 3-4 weeks to "wind down" before beginning the next training cycle.

By using the schematic presented above it is possible to achieve the highest levels of sports performance. Each period of training builds on the previous period of training and culminates in the best you can do during the competitive period. To be sure that you get the most out of each period of training you should also periodize your nutrition and recovery methods.

## Order of workouts

When working out three to six days per week, you should adhere to the following order (sequence) of training:

### 1. Technique (Skill) Learning

In order to most effectively learn new technique or to modify established technique, especially in explosive plyometrics exercises, your nervous system must be in a high energy state. In essence, you must be alert and aware of exactly what you are doing. You must be tuned into the feedback you receive and capable of making the changes needed to improve the actions desired. Because of this, technique must be first in your training before you do much physical work. Note that this is predicated on the fact that you have already developed base levels of strength and strength endurance.

## 2. Speed and Explosive Plyometric Training

If no technique work is done, speed and explosive plyometric training move to the number one position. However, before undertaking such work, it is important that you have an adequate warm-up to prepare the muscles for the high intensity encountered. If you wish to do both technique and speed or explosive plyometric work in the same session, the amount of technique work should be minimal. It should be used mainly for reinforcement of particular coordinations and as a warm-up to the speed and explosive plyometric training. Explosive plyometric exercises should always precede the speed work if the volume is kept low and done with high-intensity to prepare the muscles for the speed work. If a full explosive plyometric workout is done, there should not be any speed work or it should be limited at best.

### 3. Specialized Strength Work

All strength exercises that duplicate particular aspects of your running, cutting, throwing, or hitting technique (dynamic correspondence/specialized exercises) must be done prior to other types of strength training. At this time you must be relatively fresh and energetic so that you can concentrate on developing the muscular feel of the movements. Thus, it follows speed and plyometric work but only if you are not in a fatigue state. If you are fatigued such exercises must be done on a different day or after you have had sufficient rest.

### 4. General All-round Strength Training

Training that is general, such as all-round conditioning, and which is not specific to the joint actions or technique involved in your sport, can be done when in a fatigue state. Because of this, it follows the other types of training that require maximum levels of energy. This type of training is often done after practice. It applies mostly to novices and to some mid-level athletes. If any plyometrics are done they consist mostly of jump exercises.

### 5. Muscular Endurance/Cardiovascular Endurance

Usually these two qualities are combined but they can also be trained separately. For example, there are instances when you must work on muscular endurance as needed in cyclical events. Such workouts are localized to particular joint actions as for example, the knee drive or pawback in running. Cardiovascular work may automatically be included if it involves large body parts. For endurance athletes, jump and lead-up type plyometrics are most beneficial.

# PRINCIPLES OF TRAINING

Working out can mean many things to different people, but how you work out is critical to your development. To get the maximum results, you should adhere to the following principles of exercise:

## Individualization

Of all the principles of training, individualization is the most important. Understand that you are a unique individual. Aside from the obvious structural differences there are also physiological differences in the muscular, circulatory and nervous systems that require differences in your program. This is why you or your coach must be the one to make the final decision as to exactly which and how many exercises are needed, how many sets and reps should be done and when the exercises should be performed. Your training program should be for you and only you.

Dr. Anatoly Bondarchuk, who is considered the most outstanding Olympic coach in history, found that athletes fit into three different categories. Some show slow increases initially, gradually building up to a peak at the end of the training cycle. Others make very fast progress initially then taper off and maintain or begin to lose. Still others show moderate progress initially and then either slow down or speed up before the end of the cycle. Thus the type of athlete determines the methods to be used. This shows the importance of modifying the program according to your needs and abilities and level of play.

Do not do as is often recommended in various magazines and on the internet, do canned (set) programs that spell out what to do every day for six or more weeks. This may be of benefit to novice athletes but it will not help the serious athlete. Each program should be individualized to the specific athlete. This is why if you read my sports training books, you'll notice that I never tell the reader how many sets and repetitions to do on a daily basis or how much weight they should be handling. I do this because of the principle of individualization. Everyone should be able to determine what and how much he or she should be doing at any stage of the training. Only in this way will you be able to achieve maximum results.

Having a program handed to you may be an easy way out for many coaches and athletes, but it is not the most productive method of improving performance. In this regard I recall the words of Bondarchuk. He told me that he did not become a true coach until he learned what individualization meant. Because one program does not fit all, he had to adapt his methods for each individual athlete. As a result, he soon found that he had are at least 16 individualized periodization programs for different athletes. The key is to find what works best for you.

## Gradualness

Regardless of your exercise program or level of performance, increases in training should be very gradual. For example, if you are accustomed to doing three explosive plyometric exercises for two sets, you should not in one day change to six exercises for three sets each. Your body is not ready for such abrupt changes and because of this, injuries may occur.

## Progressiveness

In order to continually show increases in explosive power, you must progressively but gradually increase the intensity, number of exercises or number of repetitions in explosive plyometric exercises, but never more than 10 repetitions in one set. Do not do too many exercises because they can excessively fatigue the body, especially the nervous system and can lead to injury.

## Overload

Overload means that you do more than what your body is accustomed to. To increase explosiveness you must execute the plyometric exercises quicker, with more height and/or additional resistance. Doing the exercises at a faster rate of speed or in a more explosive manner applies more to high level players and used only after you have mastered the prerequisites.

## Awareness

To be aware, you should keep a record of your workouts. Record not only the intensity (weights used, height of jumps, colors of Active Cords, etc.), sets and repetitions for each exercise, but also how you feel. Make notations of what you experience, both mentally and physically.

Awareness is especially important when doing explosive plyometric exercises. It means being cognizant of what is happening to your body (what you experience) as your do these exercises. You should learn what each exercise feels like and how your body responds to it. In time, you develop a muscle memory so that when you execute the exercise you can tell immediately if it is effective and working for you. When things do not feel right, check your execution or others problems that may be interfering.

## Consistency

Consistency, which means doing the explosive plyometric exercises on a regular basis, is the key to success in any training program. If for some reason you are unable to do them for a week or so, start your exercises again upon your return using less intensity. In one or two days you should get back into the groove of doing the exercises and then return to the regular exercise program. Do not be overly concerned when situations arise that do not allow you to continue on the established program since they can be made up—if the break is not too long.

## The Training Program

Explosive plyometric training typically starts in the SPP stage and is preceded by jump (or what are commonly known as plyometric) exercises in GPP. It is at this time that the intensity of the exercises increases greatly as well as the volume. However, as you go through the SPP phase you can still include jump exercises for jump endurance etc if you are sports calls for this. Gradually change the emphasis of the early training to more sport specific strength and explosive plyometric training.

In specialized training, the goal of weight training is to increase your absolute strength and then to use this strength in the explosive plyometric exercises for further increases in explosive power. In other words, use this new strength at fast speeds or in an explosive manner to develop explosiveness. In general, the player who applies the most force at the greatest speed will typically be the better player. However, and this is most important, if you gain too much strength without literally converting it to explosive power, you will become slower.

# CHAPTER 7

# OTHER IMPORTANT FACTORS

## NUTRITION

When doing explosive plyometric training, you need to maintain your concentration throughout each exercise in the workout. Concentration is basically brain chemistry, i.e., a balance between your ability to utilize the fuel that you have taken in and your ability to convert it into the appropriate brain chemistries. All the amino acids, which are the small building blocks of proteins, are the precursors to building the brain chemistries we hear so much about today. This includes serotonin, melatonin, epinephrine, and norepinephrine as well as the other products that our brains need to be able to function well.

When you do explosive plyometrics, especially depth jumps, you use a higher amount of your brain fuels. If you are unable to replenish these fuels due to the burning up of the raw material, or not having adequate raw material, your body "stalls out." When you have a high demand, as in explosive plyometric training, and your body is unable to have the appropriate fuels to do what is needed, you will be unable to concentrate.

Emotional needs require even more nutritional support. For example, when there is a heavy emotional component in the training or game, you can burn up to 25 percent more calories than in regular play or even in some in practices. This is why it is so important to be well fortified nutritionally. Keep in mind that the minimum standards established for various vitamins and minerals are for sedentary people – not athletes. You need more than the average person and you need it in the form of natural, whole food supplements in addition to eating wholesome organic foods

## STEROIDS AND OTHER DRUGS

You have probably heard much about steroid use among athletes, not only in the high schools and colleges, but also in the professional leagues. The main reasons for such prevalent steroid use is to become a better player by becoming bigger and stronger and/or being able to recover faster from heavy workouts. To this end they are effective, but keep in mind it is only a temporary effect. When you go off the steroids you lose what you gained. By themselves, steroids do not make the physiological changes permanent or even semi-permanent except to a very limited extent. They are temporary at best.

They enable you to work harder and longer; they even change your mental outlook that drives you into working harder and longer – usually in relation to lifting heavier and in greater volume. This allows you to become bigger and stronger but you must work harder to get the results. Once you go off steroids you lose your size and strength.

In regard to explosive plyometrics, you pay a price for using steroids because your ligaments and tendons weaken. As a result you often see injuries to players. There are also many instances of the muscle (or more accurately the muscle tendon) being pulled completely off the bone. If you are an explosive athlete and involved in explosive plyometric training, steroids can be a powerful negative.

I firmly believe that steroids and/or other drugs are the reason for so many muscle pulls as for example, pulled hamstrings in running athletes. Even though the athletes may look bigger and stronger they become relatively "delicate" as it becomes increasingly difficult to prevent injury and in the long run, with heavy use, death or a major illness.

Because there is no established ormal training system in the U.S. you must rely on coaches or former players who usually teach what they were taught 20—50 years ago. This is why there is so little progress in developing a truly scientifically based training system that is effective in producing outstanding results. Sadly, most of our great athletes develop through trial and error, similar to cream rising to the top in a bottle of natural milk. Because of the masses in certain sports you will always have several outstanding athletes.

If you train scientifically, there is little to no need to use steroids. One of the biggest myths is that you need steroids to be a good athlete. Probably the main reason is the drug use confessions by high-level athletes giving the erroneous message that the only way to be great is to use steroids. As a result, many players still believe in the use of steroids that are used in almost all sports – even golf, that is now calling for drug testing! It will continue this way until coaches and athletes learn there are more effective and safer ways of training.

Another major problem stemming from steroid use is that you not only become bigger and stronger, but in time, also slower. This is especially bad for explosive and speed-oriented athletes. Being slow may be great for some football linemen, bodybuilders and powerlifters, but not for running athletes, or those who must jump high, execute short bursts of speed, changes in direction and other explosive actions. Steroids will hinder your performance and make you more prone to injury.

# RECOVERY

In recent years, athletes have been increasing the number of days that they work out in addition to using more voluminous and intense physical loads which includes more explosive plyometric training. Because of this, many are overtraining, getting injured, feeling tired, and lacking energy.

It appears to be a paradox. You must keep increasing the amount and intensity of training in order to get greater gains in explosive power and strength. But by so doing, you are depleting your body to such an extent that it is incapable of physically recuperating to be able to handle more such loads. The body undergoes much greater stress than previously. This in turn results in greater fatigue, poorer immune system functioning and overtraining. Because of this, athletes must look to other means to help recuperate the body so that it, in turn, can handle the loads more effectively.

For example, you must get more rest to allow for sufficient recuperation between workouts. Steroids are used for restoration, but the benefits of steroids are greatly outweighed by their negative effects. In the long run, steroids are more detrimental to not only your training, but also your health.

Using natural restorative methods are more effective than steroids, and may even improve your health. The use of natural ways of restoring the body, i.e. getting the body recovered and ready for more work as soon as possible, is gaining greater recognition by athletes and coaches. By helping the body to recover faster after workouts you can actually increase the amount of work that can be done.

Natural methods of restoration have been used in the Eastern Bloc countries for many decades. In these countries the athletes, coaches and scientists found that systematic employment of recovery methods makes it possible to significantly increase (sharply, in some cases) the volume and intensity of training. In addition, the number of injuries and ailments that occur to an athlete's skeletal-muscular system, not only does not increase, but is reduced. This is especially true when doing explosive plyometrics. As brought out previously, explosive plyometrics are very stressful. The better and faster you can recover, the more effective will be your training.

Unskillful use of recovery methods can lead to marked increases in the amount of training work and yet not provide a corresponding training effect. Because of this, it is important to know how to combine the workouts with recovery at different stages of training. Keep in mind that each cycle of training should start after a period of rest and recovery.

For more information on the different recovery methods read *Russian Sports Restoration and Massage*. It gives examples of many different methods, how and when they are used with different athletes and which supplements can be used to speed your recovery. It is available at *DrYessis.com* under sports training books.

# About the Author
# Dr. Michael Yessis

Dr. Michael Yessis received his Ph.D. from the University of Southern California and his B.S. and M.S. from City University of New York. He is president of Sports Training, Inc., a diverse sports and fitness company and Professor Emeritus at California State University, Fullerton, where he was a multi-sports specialist in biomechanics (technique analysis) and sports conditioning and training. In addition, he is the foremost U.S. expert on Russian training methods.

In his work, Dr. Yessis has done thousands of visual biomechanical analyses of basic sports skills. He is the prominent voice in the U.S. recognizing the need for technique analysis in addition to physical conditioning to improve athletic performance. He has developed many unique specialized strength and explosive exercises that unite technique with development of the physical abilities.

He has served as training and technique consultant to several Olympic and professional sports teams and athletes, including the L.A. baseball teams, L.A. Rams and L.A. Raiders football clubs, Natadore Diving Team, and the U.S. Men's Volleyball Team. He has also successfully trained national and state champions in different sports incorporating Russian techniques with his own unique exercises and training programs.

Dr. Yessis has written 16 original books which include best sellers such as *Secrets of Russian Sports Fitness and Training*, *Kinesiology of Exercise*, *Explosive Running,* and *Build A Better Athlete.* He has also been translating Russian sports training information for over 40 years. Most of his translations have appeared in the *Soviet Sports Review*, later known as the *Fitness and Sports Review International,* that were published for almost 30 years. In recent years, he has translated books by Dr. Anatoly Bondarchuk (*Transfer of Training 1* and *2*), Dr. Yuri Verkhoshansky (*Specialized Strength Training*), and Dr. Vladimir Issurin (*Block Periodization* and *Principles and Basics of Advanced Athletic Training*).

He has written more than 2,000 articles on fitness and sports training that have appeared in magazines such as *Muscle and Fitness, Men's Fitness, Scholastic Coach, Fitness Management, National Strength and Conditioning Association Journal, Peak Running, Running Times* and *Volleyball*. In addition, he has completed six DVD's; Exercise Mastery, Developing a Quarterback's Arm and Strength, Explosive Golf, Specialized Strength and Explosive Exercises for Baseball, Explosive Tennis and Specialized Strength and Explosive Exercises for Softball.

His popular website, DrYessis.com, is visited by many people ranging from scientists and university professors to coaches, athletes and fitness buffs. Most frequently viewed are his store with its unique books and products and his blogs that address the latest in sports training and current sports news for all sports.

Made in the USA
Columbia, SC
24 March 2020